the Other Side of Forgiveness

the Other Side *of* Forgiveness

HOW TO FIND RELEASE FROM THE PRISON OF YOUR PAST

DIONNEA SEALS, LPC

CHICAGO, ILLINOIS

© 2019 by Dionnea Seals
Published by Gabuchi Publishing House
Gabuchi Publishing House
1440 W. Taylor Street #752
Chicago, IL 60607
www.dionneaseals.com

Printed in the United States of America
All rights reserved. This book or any portion thereof may not be reproduced or used in any manner whatsoever including photocopying, recording, or other electronic or mechanical methods, without the express written permission of the publisher except for the use of brief quotations in a book review.

Library of Congress Control Number:2019909208

ISBN Print 13: 978-0-9988670-2-1
ISBN E-Book 13: 978-0-9988670-3-8
ISBN Audiobook 13: 978-0-9988670-4-5

Publisher's Cataloging-In-Publication Data
(Prepared by The Donohue Group, Inc.)

Names: Seals, Dionnea, author.
Title: The other side of forgiveness : how to find release from the prison
    of your past / Dionnea Seals, LPC.
Description: First edition. | Chicago, Illinois : Gabuchi Publishing
    House, 2019. | Includes bibliographical references and index.
Identifiers: ISBN 9780998867021 (print) | ISBN 9780998867038 (ebook)
Subjects: LCSH: Forgiveness--Religious aspects--Christianity. | Seals,
    Dionnea--Religion. | Spiritual healing. | Christian life.
Classification: LCC BV4647.F55 S43 2019 (print) | LCC BV4647.F55 (ebook) |
    DDC 234.5--dc23

All Scripture quotations, unless otherwise indicated, are taken from the Holy Bible, New International Version®, NIV®. Copyright ©1973, 1978, 1984, 2011 by Biblica, Inc.™ Used by permission of Zondervan. All rights reserved worldwide. www.zondervan.com The "NIV" and "New International Version" are trademarks registered in the United States Patent and Trademark Office by Biblica, Inc.™

Scriptures marked ESV are taken from the THE HOLY BIBLE, ENGLISH STANDARD VERSION (ESV): Scriptures taken from THE HOLY BIBLE, ENGLISH STANDARD VERSION ®Copyright© 2001 by Crossway, a publishing ministry of Good News Publishers. Used by permission.

Scriptures marked NLT are taken from the HOLY BIBLE, NEW LIVING TRANSLATION (NLT): Scriptures taken from the HOLY BIBLE, NEW LIVING TRANSLATION, Copyright© 1996, 2004, 2007 by Tyndale House Foundation. Used by permission of Tyndale House Publishers, Inc., Carol Stream, Illinois 60188. All rights reserved. Used by permission.

Scriptures marked NKJV are taken from the NEW KING JAMES VERSION (NKJV): Scripture taken from the NEW KING JAMES VERSION®. Copyright© 1982 by Thomas Nelson, Inc. Used by permission. All rights reserved.

Scripture quotations marked NASB are taken from the New American Standard Bible ®, copyright ©1960, 1962, 1963, 1968, 1971, 1972, 1973, 1975, 1977, 1995 by The Lockman Foundation. Used by permission. (www.Lockman.org)

Scripture quotations marked (AMP) are taken from the Amplified Bible, Copyright © 2015 by The Lockman Foundation. Used by permission.

Editor, Ashley Casteel

Cover Design by Gabuchi Publishing House

First Edition, 2019
10 9 8 7 6 5 4 3 2

Dedication

This book is dedicated to all those who struggle to forgive and heal.

The Spirit of the Sovereign Lord is on me, because the Lord has anointed me to proclaim good tidings to the poor; He has sent me to heal the brokenhearted, to proclaim liberty for the captives and the opening of the prison to those who are bound.

Isaiah 61:1 NKJV

Contents

	Introduction	11
1.	Wake-Up Call	17
2.	What's Your Excuse	31
3.	Get to the Root	47
4.	When Your Expectations are Shattered	59
5.	When You've Been Dropped	71
6.	When the Hurt is Close	89
7.	When it Doesn't Make Sense	109
8.	When Grace and Mercy Follow Me	127
9.	At the Cross	145
	Contract	161
	Frequently Asked Questions	163
	Notes	178
	Acknowledgments	179
	About the Author	180

Introduction

YOU CAN FORGIVE. It's no coincidence that you were drawn to this book. It's no accident that you chose to read this book. Like me (and many others), you've questioned whether you can forgive. You know that you should, but *how* do you get to the place of forgiveness? And how do you *stay* there? It may seem daunting, but I want to start by saying you've made the right choice. By choosing this book, you've acknowledged that change is needed. And that's precisely where you're supposed to begin.

Unforgiveness is defined by Merriam-Webster as "being unwilling or unable to forgive. Having or making no allowance for error or weakness." Another definition is "a grudge against someone who has offended you." No matter how you characterize it, the universal perception of unforgiveness is negative, as evidenced by the wounds we carry and the stories we tell about its devastating impacts. In fact, unforgiveness is downright poisonous, wreaking havoc on our bodies by causing us to feel weighted and drained. According to the Mayo Clinic, the emotional toll of unforgiveness can contribute to chronic pain, heart disease, cancer, hypertension, and many other physical conditions. Spiritually, unforgiveness can also do grave damage—from hindering our prayers to spawning generational curses, emotional/mental struggles, and financial instability.

Unforgiveness is a serious issue, and I want to help you let it go.

HOW TO USE THIS BOOK

Whether young or old, Christian or not, spiritually mature or a new believer, forgiveness is for all. I've found that to grasp the origins of unforgiveness fully, the point at which it manifested in humanity and the reason why it persists, there is only one place to look. It's the same place that gives us the prescription for offense and emotional healing. That place is the Bible.

The Word of God, inspired by the Holy Spirit and written by men, is filled with timeless accounts of individuals who've experienced heartbreaks, setbacks, triumphs, and tragedies. Many

Introduction

biblical figures both suffered the deep wounds of unforgiveness and found freedom in the redemptive power of forgiveness as they endured God's testing, family conflicts, and plans that unraveled. Through their example, we discover the beauty of lives transformed. No other book has the power to convict and heal at the same time. This sword, also known as the Bible, is lifesaving.

> For the word of God is alive and powerful. It is sharper than the sharpest two-edged sword, cutting between soul and spirit, between joint and marrow. It exposes our innermost thoughts and desires. Nothing in all creation is hidden from God. Everything is naked and exposed before his eyes, and he is the one to whom we are accountable.
>
> Hebrews 4:12–13 NLT

In this book I will share with you the insights and revelations that the Holy Spirit revealed to me as I struggled to get to the other side of forgiveness. He helped me remember stories about individuals in the Bible who dealt with the same emotional obstacles and doubts on their journeys. As you read, you'll notice similarities to your own life. But not only that, you'll better understand how they, and I, overcame unforgiveness by God's strength—and how you can too. You'll be introduced to their stories, relate to their circumstances, and gain insight into how God shaped their lives for your sake. This prolific and authoritative book, written thousands of years ago, is still relevant today. The Bible has been my lifeline on my journey of healing. You'll also read about some of my personal experiences that God highlighted as I struggled to forgive. I urge you to go through each chapter with the expectation that God will meet you where you are, take you to new levels in Him, and help you get to the other side of forgiveness.

As a Licensed Professional Counselor, I meet clients who tell me their stories, and I've realized that whether they're nine years old or fifty-nine, they often share a common narrative: Pain from past experiences continues to block their future hopes. I have faith that this book will grace you with care, compassion, and hope. When your heart is hurting from an offense, healing may happen all at once or gradually over a period of time. But no matter how long it takes, know that you *can* get to the other side.

At the end of each chapter, you'll find **Take A Moment** sections that I've developed to help you **Reflect** on what you've read and experienced. Simple prompts for self-exploration are intended to reveal ways to integrate what you've read and provide insights into your personal experiences. You'll also be called to **Act** by taking simple steps that will assist you in moving forward. Lastly, each closing **Prayer** will encourage your growth and support your healing. Prayers are investments in your future. They are never futile and can be powerful tools that will help you along your journey. Prayer is your connection and lifeline to the Holy Spirit, who is always available and ready to help.

At the end of this book, you may decide that additional counseling would benefit your journey to healing. Or, you may realize this book adequately complements what you're currently

Introduction

doing. No matter what you choose to do, I am confident that God, our Great Physician, will confirm what you need and how you should go about this process.

Not only do I want you to get to the other side of forgiveness, but my desire is also for you to maintain an attitude that's free of offense. Jesus sees your brokenness and your pain, and He wants this for you.

He has a remedy. He *is* the cure.

Let's get real. Let's deal and let's heal.

> *The LORD is close to the brokenhearted*
> *and saves those who are crushed in spirit.*
>
> *Psalm 34:18*

If forgiveness were easy,

everyone would do it.

chapter 1

Wake-Up Call

"You have dwelt long enough at this mountain."

~Deuteronomy 1:6 NKJV

I SHOULD HAVE seen this day coming. It made perfect sense that God would ask me to do what I thought was impossible. *I can't believe the Holy Spirit just checked me,* I thought. My laughter was mixed with embarrassment and nervousness at what I had just heard from God. I immediately wanted to hide from Him, as though I were in the Garden like Adam and Eve. My eyes had been opened, and I knew what had to be done. But how? I wanted to avoid Him, but I could not. My vulnerability had been exposed, but I felt safe enough to let my guard down with the One who knew me better than

I know myself. My lips wanted to say yes to His request; to fully uncover and deal with an issue that had plagued me for years. He had called me out and exposed what was invisible to others, and His timing was amazing.

For two months, frantic searches around the house for the notes to my next book turned up nothing. I realize now that not finding my detailed outline was no coincidence at all. God was making it clear what *He* wanted me to focus on—and it took me by surprise. He was ordering my steps to write, but not what I wanted. Rather, it was the writing He knew I needed to do. Months prior, signs confirming His will interrupted my daily routine. I couldn't escape nudges from the Holy Spirit as He called me to confront and deal with a dilemma that had me bound.

"Why are you still holding on to this? Forgive and let it go." My questions and skepticism only seemed to intensify, but as much as I wanted to ignore it, I couldn't escape His request anymore. Like repeated taps on the shoulder from the Holy Spirit, recurring dreams of guidance and correction further confirmed His calling to write a new song on my heart. He was pleading for me to change from the inside out. I knew my heart needed transformation, but I didn't know to what extent. Even *I* caught myself asking the same question: *Why are you still holding on? Aren't you tired?* My dysfunctional attachment to past offenses was no longer feasible or conducive to where I wanted to be. As cliché as it sounds, I was sick and tired of being sick and tired. I wanted to soar and stop feeling wounded. I wanted to be in control instead of being controlled. The

desire to pursue personal growth tugged at my mind. However, I didn't know *how* to let the offenses that plagued me go. Finally, my heart was ripe enough to accept the seeds He desired to plant. He knew I was ready to get real with my pain and unravel all that came along with it.

My full-circle moment came at a time when I was questioning God's delay in sending me my soul mate. *Lord, what's taking so long? Where is the person you have for me?* Interestingly, my proverbial date with destiny happened on social media. One night, I was searching for more than something to entertain me. I desired to be encouraged through a song or word from God. I browsed YouTube for a video that would inspire me to keep waiting on God's timing for marriage. The title of one video caught me by surprise: "A Big Sign You're Not Ready for Marriage." It was the opposite of what I was searching for, but I couldn't ignore it.

With caution and intrigue, I reread the title of the video before clicking the link. *Surely,* I thought, *this video won't encourage me.* But curiosity held me captive. I wanted to know the perspective of its creator. I even began thinking about my rebuttal (before I'd even watched the video, mind you). I was fed up with my singleness and those who failed miserably at attempting to encourage singles in their waiting. *Hmmm,* I wondered, *what could be "the sign?"* Curiosity made me click on the video, but something else kept my eyes glued and ears alert to what the young woman onscreen had to say. To my surprise, God lovingly used this video as an impromptu counseling session . . . for me. It was the climax of what He'd been saying to me all year. Repeated dreams, stirrings in my heart, and revelations had led me to this moment.

As I continued to watch the video, the woman's words were all too familiar and confirmed what God had clearly shown me in a dream: Offense would hinder Him from bringing the blessing of marriage into my life. But even though I recognized this as truth in my heart, my mind gave me reasons why I could not accept it. Like a defense lawyer, I looked at all angles and sides of the issue in search of evidence to support my theory that unforgiveness was too difficult to erase or overcome.

I made a list of all my grudges—thirteen, to be exact. Only thirteen. It wasn't the first time I'd made such a list, and I reflected on the lists I'd made in years past. Admittedly, it was shorter than it had ever been. Of course, it could have been longer, had I continued to recall more things in the past. However, I elected to stop counting after thirteen. God knew there was more. I couldn't fool Him. What hadn't changed was my motivation to "get over it." My list of thirteen grudges was a revelation. No wonder I experienced unease and felt emotionally overwhelmed. At that moment, I became grossly uncomfortable with the weight of the invisible baggage I'd been carrying for so long. For years, my attempts to break free from the grip of offense were unsuccessful. I vowed over and over again in my journal to turn the page and move forward in the new year, but it never happened.

I should have known that change was on the horizon. All that week, God kept confirming my need to forgive. The invisible weight of the pain I carried began affecting more areas of my life than I'd thought. Did I want to heal? Yes. But how? I desired to wake up and find my hurt removed miraculously. However, I thought the process would require more than I could give. Or would it? Suddenly there was no more confusion on my end. Yes, I wanted to heal.

That video about marital readiness brought out questions and anger in me I didn't know I'd been harboring. God confronted me, and I didn't like it one bit. "Forgive as God has forgiven you," the woman had said. Abruptly, I stopped the video and began to get defensive with God. In hindsight, my rebuttal was foolish and comical. Did I really think that my argument would override His wisdom? Growing up in church, I'd heard it all before—all the reasons why we should forgive. Biblically based explanations on the importance of forgiveness. And I believed them. However, forgiveness is much easier said than done, and the case I made to God conveyed that sentiment.

"But God, of course *You* have the power to forgive—You're *God!*" Before I had a chance to finish the sentence, the Holy Spirit quickly responded and shut. Me. Down.

"Yes, I'm God and have the power to forgive. But you have *access* to My power."

How could anyone devise a comeback after a response like that? With my head hung in defeat, I knew I couldn't deny what my ears and heart had heard. His remedy for letting go made complete sense, and I waved my white flag of surrender. "Okay God, you're right, and I'm ready. Let's get to the root of my issue."

In June 2017, God gave me a dream in which He answered the question that had been weighing on my mind: *God, what's taking so long?* My bold question contained all the frustration and curiosity of someone who knew the promise would come. However, I wanted to understand what was going on behind the scenes. The answer He gave shocked me. "Your friend is on the other side of forgiveness." *The other side of forgiveness?* I laid in bed reflecting on what I'd just heard and seen. Then I laughed. Well, sort of. To my surprise, God's response had more to do with *me* than I anticipated. I woke up with mixed feelings about what had just occurred. *God, that's your answer? Are you sure?* I couldn't believe it, but I knew I needed to own it.

In addition to waiting on His perfect timing, I had to do something to receive His promise. The ball was in my hands, and I didn't know what to do with it. I knew what should happen, but I had difficulty in believing that I could do it.

God speaks in so many ways, though dreams have become His primary way of communicating with me as of late. Correction, guidance, promises, and warnings in dreams were some of His other means of communication that I'd grown accustomed to as a child. Through this specific dream, God provided strategic insight and revelation into what I needed in order to get to the other side of forgiveness. He gave me the antidote to my ailment. A resolution was in sight–that is, if I wanted to obtain the promise and truly desired to press delete on my past.

Writing this book has challenged my heart, confronted my resistance, and highlighted *my* need for grace. All my love for Jesus and God's Word did not diminish the fact that I lacked mercy for others. I was the walking wounded. No, I was not seeking revenge, nor did I want others to experience pain. But I wanted apologies and recognition from my offenders. I longed to turn back the hands of time and rewrite my steps and part in the story. I lived in regret and lounged in the memories of yesterday.

If only I could start over with the knowledge I have now. Would I?

My regrets were clouded by pain and filtered through mournful thoughts. *If only I'd never met them, then I wouldn't be going through this. If only I had made better decisions.* If. Only. However, some beauty can be found in the messiness of life—especially when you give God the pen to rewrite your story. Sometimes, walking along the muddy road is the only way to get to the beautiful meadow.

I share my revelations from God as a student who has not reached a state of perfection. But, as someone who is relying on the One for continual renewal, revelations, and strength. The process of becoming more like Christ is a journey.

I realize this subject is a silent epidemic, especially in the church. We're quick to make prayer requests about negative medical prognoses, and we're always willing to provide testimonials about deliverance, as we should. But rarely do we hear others talk about their deliverance from unforgiveness. Seldom do we hear someone say, "I'm *suffering* from unforgiveness," or "The grudge I've been holding on to has been keeping me captive."

It takes courage and vulnerability to admit your ownership of a grudge. We may offer some pat answers and provide examples from Scripture stating why forgiveness is essential. However, many still find themselves going in circles, unable to get to the other side.

No, it's not easy to talk about the subject, because of the attachment to deep issues that are long buried. It's difficult to admit that we've become used to wearing a mask. But there's a pain, hurt, and anger behind the facade. And dare I say, sometimes we're angry at God. The woman in church who loves God but can't seem to find her way out of the endless cycle of unforgiveness. Yes, I can relate because I *was* that woman.

So many times I tried to let the offense go. For years I'd attempted to forgive on my own. From creating lists of those who had wronged me and why, to writing a letter to my enemy, nothing seemed to work. I was missing key ingredients to make the pain go away. I didn't know how to do it, and truth be told, I wasn't too sure if I wanted to. So used to keeping score, my mental tallies provided me with unhealthy comforts. I didn't know how much pain I was causing myself. I wasn't aware that every score kept or mentioned was essentially a grave I was digging for myself. But the wounded healer, Jesus, knew. And He wanted more than attempts from me. He desired determination and commitment coupled with action. He desired that I plug into Him—the ultimate power source that could defeat unforgiveness and heal every pain. And that's what He wants for you. God has given you a wake-up call. It's time to stop sweeping your issues under the rug. It's time to stop placing a band-aid on wounds that are not healing properly. It's time to stop using scriptures without power and without believing them. It's long overdue that you stop hiding behind a mask of good health when you're bleeding on the inside. It's time to be honest about what hurts you, what keeps bothering you, and why. It's time to face the baggage of your past and intentionally unpack it. You've been in prison way too long. You're standing inside the cell, yet holding the key for your release.

Isn't it time to turn the page in your story?

"I can't forgive them. I'll never forgive them for that. What they did to me is unforgivable." I'm sure at some point you've caught yourself saying something to this effect. Emotions may consume you because of what you've gone through. Here's a stark reality: It takes more intentionality to recall the wounds and offense you've endured than you may realize. The past is alive in our memories. Passwords to unlock or retrieve them aren't necessary. Sometimes, past recollections show up spontaneously or are triggered by situations or people. No, you never forget when or how you were wounded—no matter how long ago the memory was buried.

But God has a lot to say when it comes to recalling the past. Aside from remembering the good times experienced with loved ones and friends, God gives us a few other reasons why recalling the past is beneficial:

1. **To remind us what *not* to do:**

   "Remember what happened to Lot's Wife!"

   Luke 17:32 NLT

Lot's wife turned into a pillar of salt after the angels gave explicit instructions to flee their home in Sodom and Gomorrah and not look back.

> And we must not engage in sexual immorality as some of them did, causing 23,000 of them to die in one day. Nor should we put Christ to the test, as some of them did and then died from snakebites. And don't grumble as some of them did, and then were destroyed by the angel of death. These things happened to them as examples for us. They were written down to warn us who lives at the end of the age.
>
> 1 Corinthians 10:8–11 NLT

A solemn warning was given to the early church, reminding them not to follow the behaviors of the children of Israel during their time in the wilderness.

2. **To encourage us to remember how He's constant and faithful in our lives.**

   For forty years I led you through the wilderness, yet your clothes and sandals did not wear out.

   Deuteronomy 29:5 NLT

God's resources were always abundant for the children of Israel. They lacked nothing, even during moments of difficulty.

If you've never recalled your past for any of these reasons, I believe you're missing the essence and purpose of God using what happened to your benefit. You've allowed your wounds to cloud your view of the future, hold your thoughts hostage, and prevent you from moving forward.

Dear friend, you've accomplished this through offense. It's amazing how years can pass by, yet the details and emotions of what happened can still seem so vivid, as though it occurred yesterday. Make no mistake about it—the past can be a powerful prison.

As you continue to answer the call to examine your past, your future is asking, *What about me?* What if this mountain of unforgiveness is standing in the way of your dreams, your physical or emotional healing, a marriage restored, or a satisfied heart? What if the very thing you've been waiting for were within reach? The very thing God has promised you? What if forgiveness is the key to ushering in the abundant life you've been promised? *What if?*

If unforgiveness is a choice in response to your circumstances, then choosing forgiveness is the key that will unlock your door of destiny.

It's your time. It's your time to change the script of your story.

Everybody has a story. What I discovered is that even though our experiences may define us at any given moment, it is our responsibility to decide if those events will be the ultimate guiding force in our lives. Don't let unforgiveness and pain have the final say in your life. You owe it to yourself and others to make the necessary changes to overcome these obstacles. Most of all, you owe it to God.

The One who created you and made you to thrive. Dear friend, you cannot succeed in life when you've allowed yourself to be weighed down. You get one shot at life. Make it count by unlocking the door to your prison and running for your life!

The Forgiving Tip #1

When you don't forgive, you settle for a life of mediocrity. Don't settle when God has called you to soar. He's calling you higher. Answer the call.

Reflection Scripture

"Look! I stand at the door and knock. If you hear my voice and open the door, I will come in, and we will share a meal together as friends."
Revelation 3:20 NLT

❧ Take A Moment ❧

Reflect

1. Forgiveness is:
2. Healing is:
3. I am offended by:
4. The emotion(s) I feel from the offense is:

Act

- Get real and acknowledge your offense and hurt to Christ. If you have to, write it out.
- Pray and ask God to reveal the hidden things within your heart that may hinder you from thriving in life.

Prayer

Dear heavenly Father,

Thank You for my life. Thank You for illuminating the deep issues of my heart to me and thank You for wanting better for me. I realize that I've been wounded for a long time and standing in the way of my need to forgive. For too long I've tried to do it my way, only to fall short. Thank You for wanting the best for me. To soar like an eagle and thrive instead of merely surviving in life. The road ahead seems scary, and I don't know which way to go. Please help me walk this road of forgiveness. I'm ready to live the best life that You've ordained for me. I don't want to give another second or thought to my past without knowing what to do with the residual pain. You said in Your Word that I can cast my cares on You and that nothing is too hard for You to deal with. Forgiveness seems impossible, but I know that with You, all things are possible! Lord, You've called me out so that You can bring me in—closer to You and focused on things ahead. Lord, I'm ready to walk this journey of forgiveness and healing. Have Your way in me.

In Jesus's name,

Amen

chapter 2

What's Your Excuse?

Life is about choices, and every choice has a consequence.

~Reverend Robert Seals

AT SOME POINT the man at the pool of Bethesda stopped trying. He resigned himself to his circumstances and merely hoped that he could still get well without making an effort. He watched from the sidelines as others received what he longed for—healing. He observed in defeat and tolerated his dilemma. We're unsure of how he arrived there, or how long he'd made attempts to get help. However, one question from Jesus revealed that his physical suffering was the least of his worries. Often, in our quest to heal and forgive, complacency blocks our view as we fail to see the obvious.

This man had no name, but we're introduced to him by his location. His identity is forever tied to the space he occupied, the opportunities he'd missed, and his infamous response to a life-changing question. Like others, he waited for his chance to be healed. At the stirring of waters, people who were sick, blind, lame, or paralyzed hoped that it would be their turn for healing. Everyone longed for a miracle, but not all were given their breakthrough at the pool of Bethesda. Throughout the Bible, only a handful of people are identified according to their illness. In this case, the crisis of the man at the pool became his identity—to the point that he could not answer a question from Jesus with a simple yes or no.

His story is a standout among the healings Jesus performed that were recorded in the Bible. We don't know how long the man sat there waiting at the pool, but we do know he'd suffered from sickness for thirty-eight years. The details of his diagnosis remain unknown, except that it compromised his ability to walk. He sat and watched others received their healing when the waters were stirred. After thirty-eight long years, his questions of *when* healing would arrive may have turned into questions of *if* healing would arrive. Quiet acceptance of his condition could have silenced the hope he once had. With the passage of time, his attitude about his illness likely developed into a way of life.

How about you? Have your issues of unforgiveness allowed complacency and hopelessness to gain the upper hand in your life?

His story doesn't have any plot twists or drama like others in the Bible, but the timeless question Jesus confronted him with continues to challenge us to this day. Of all the miracles and healings performed by Jesus, there's only one account in which Jesus seemingly asks a rhetorical question.

When Jesus saw him lying there, and knew he had already been in that condition a long time, He said to him, "Do you want to be made well?" (John 5:6 NKJV)

At first glance, some might be startled to hear the One who has the power to heal ask a man—who *needed* healing—if he *wanted* to be healed. But if we look again, the question was intended to get to matters of the heart and not solely physical healing. That question from Jesus seems to imply that the man had some choice and responsibility regarding his infirmary. It makes us question whether he really had to endure thirty-eight years of sickness. It gives us pause to wonder whether his illness existed longer than it should have. Did this man have the answer to his ailment all along?

Jesus never asks a question without knowing the answer. He never asks for the sake of finding out. Instead, His questions encourage us to look within, challenging us to reflect and rethink our wants while acknowledging our actual needs. The man at the pool wanted physical healing, but his primary needs included a renewed mind and transformed heart. For those who find themselves digging their way out from offense and going through life as spectators rather than participants, Jesus still asks, "Do you want to be made whole?"

Do you want to forgive?

Do you want your emotions from offense healed?

Aren't you tired of hurting?

Aren't you tired of playing the blame game?

Do you want to stop keeping score?

Do you want to enjoy your life?

Do you want to sit in the pool of your pain?

Do you want help from the One who has the power to help?

Do you want to do your part and take the first step?

Do you want what happened to keep you bound?

Do you want to grow from this?

Do you want to spend another moment living a life of mediocrity?

How badly do you want forgiveness and healing?

Will you respond to Jesus in the same way that the man at the pool of Bethesda did?

The sick man answered him, "Sir, I have no man to put me in the pool when the water is stirred up; but while I am coming, another steps down before me." (John 5:7 NKJV)

His admission that he was waiting for someone to place him in the water when it was stirred gives us some insight into his active and passive response. He actively waited for change to happen *to* him. However, he was passive about *how* it would happen.

The man's response also provides a clue as to why his illness had lasted so long. Instead of answering with a simple yes, he answered with an excuse for *why* healing had appeared to escape his grasp. The Bible lets us know that before Jesus came to the pool, He went to other places in Jerusalem. Therefore, we can infer with confidence that Jesus's ministry and miracles were known all over. However, this man at the pool answered with "Sir." He seemed to be unaware of who he was talking to and what was possible for him. After thirty-eight years, his uncomfortable ailment became part of him. It had now shaped his perspective on life. He allowed his circumstance to diminish his hope, and he believed that his healing was dependent on others. Unbeknownst to him, that question from Jesus was a setup for so much more. And Jesus continues to ask the same question of us when we rehash our past hurts.

His infamous question reveals three truths:
- Not everyone desires to get well.
- Those who want to get well may not know how.
- Those who wish to get well may be tired of waiting and trying.

If any of these truths resonate with you, believing that change will come is only half the battle.

The Bible doesn't say how long the man stayed at the pool waiting. However, after thirty-eight years of illness, fear may have added to his hope deferred, and that fear may have contributed to his inaction and complacency.

As much as we desire change, we also fear the unknown—along with hope, trying, and believing that we can rise above unforgiveness and be made whole. At times it's tempting to give in to those fears and give up. Because overcoming offense and getting to the other side of forgiveness takes work.

We give up too soon.

We doubt.

We pray once or a couple of times and give up.

We don't pray *and* fast.

We don't change our thinking.

We don't change our behavior.

We don't pray the right prayers.

We don't pray for our enemies.

As much as we want it, we may secretly fear getting to the other side. We fear it because holding on to grudges has consumed us, become familiar, and given us false comfort in unhealthy ways.

I say, no more.

Let's revisit what the man at the pool of Bethesda said one more time: "The sick man answered him, 'Sir, I have no man to put me in the pool when the water is stirred up; but while I am coming, another steps down before me' " (John 5:7 NKJV).

His response gives us the action plan we need to get to the other side of forgiveness and find release from the prison of our past. If we want to heal, we need to get our lives in order, starting with:

Our Speech.

Our Thoughts.

Our Actions.

YOUR SPEECH

His statement contained more than words. It also revealed the condition of his heart. On that subject Matthew 12:34 (NKJV) says, "Out of the abundance of the heart the mouth speaks." God's Word also says, "Death and life are in the power of the tongue, and those who love it and indulge it will eat its fruit and bear the consequences of their words" (Proverbs 18:21 AMP). If your heart is evil, critical, filled with unbelief, jealousy, hatred, etc., your mouth will produce like words. What are you believing and saying about your experience?

YOUR THOUGHTS

Are you proactive when it comes to your thought life? As the man at the pool of Bethesda yearned for healing, his thoughts played a key role. Based on his response to Jesus, we can assume he wasn't thinking thoughts of hope and faith for healing. Instead of resisting doubts, his mind settled there. Three key verses caution and assist us concerning our thought life:

- For as he thinks in his heart, so is he. (Proverbs 23:7 NKJV)
- We demolish arguments and every pretension that sets itself up against the knowledge of God, and we take captive every thought to make it obedient to Christ. (2 Corinthians 10:5)
- Do not be conformed to this world, but be transformed by the renewal of your mind. (Romans 12:2 ESV)

We are responsible for what we allow into our minds. Do you let words or images take up residence that should not be there? Are you able to distinguish whether your thoughts are from God or the enemy? Your life cannot be changed if your mind has not been conditioned to stop negative thoughts in their tracks and be transformed.

YOUR ACTIONS

If you're trying to forgive and heal from emotional wounds, weakening your faith will keep you in the same place—just like the man at the pool of Bethesda. The Bible says:

> What good is it, my brothers and sisters, if someone claims to have faith but has no deeds? Can such faith save them? Suppose a brother or a sister is without clothes and daily food. If one of you says to them, "Go in peace; keep warm and well fed," but does nothing about their physical needs, what good is it? In the same way, faith by itself, if it is not accompanied by action, is dead. (James 2:14–17)

When Jesus asked the man at the pool of Bethesda if he wanted to be healed, the man failed to see his resource. How many resources has God made available to you that you're not utilizing? For example, having a trusted inner circle to confide in and lean on will be instrumental to your healing. Do you have a church home? Are you attending regularly? Resources may come through healing or deliverance ministries within your local church, leadership within the church, or ministries that are not connected to the church you attend. Have you been inquiring?

COUNSELING

I had to be honest and ask myself: Was I doing all that I could to forgive and heal my emotions? Or was I resorting to wishful thinking? I couldn't just wish the offenses away. I had to be intentional. Consistently intentional about forgiveness. I can recall a conversation that I had years ago with my friend, an older woman of faith. Although she's no longer alive, her sound advice proved to be instrumental in my life.

I confided in her about a potential romantic dilemma that had taken a wrong turn. I had said something that embarrassed and offended a young man. I don't recall exactly what it was, but by his reaction, I knew that my words were piercing. Unintentionally, I had hurt him—in front of others, no less. After telling my friend—the one who prayed for me and with me, and the one who held me accountable—she spoke the truth that I needed to hear: "Ms. Seals, it keeps coming up because it hasn't been healed."

I knew exactly what she meant. I had dragged into my present the offense and pain from a past relationship I'd had as a teen and into young adulthood. I still carried an experience from that relationship that I never adequately dealt with. Because I did not heal, my offense and pain projected onto others.

My friend suggested that counseling would help me deal with the root of my issues. As a devout Christian woman who loved and trusted God, she knew that God had positioned individuals in counselor roles with the intellectual and professional training and spiritual insight to help me even more than she could. And she was right. My friend introduced me to Christian counseling. Not only did she recognize my need to forgive, but she also gave me confidence in my decision to attend counseling.

I, along with many believers, have questioned whether going to counseling is a betrayal to Christ and personal faith. And many still have that question today. I wondered if, by going to counseling, I was denying God's power and what He could do. But as my friend explained, God uses different methods that are aligned with His will to help individuals heal. It is by His power that healing occurs and according to His means.

Her words not only helped me decide to attend, but they also confirmed what God had already shown me in a dream. Did I heal and "get over it" right away? No. But counseling planted seeds of courage in me to talk about things I'd kept suppressed for years. My initial counseling experience gave me the confidence to vocalize my wounds, and also the tools I needed to understand how my past had bled into my present. Confronting those wounds were my initial first steps. The process of healing became a journey over time. Christian counseling helped me chip away at the old injuries that were impairing my present. That was a critical turning point in my life.

God may be calling you to walk out this process through counseling. Are you apprehensive about doing so? Did you start to attend but end the session early? We're never meant to heal or go through life alone. When there's someone there to listen, hold you accountable, and pray with/for you, healing may happen more rapidly. Ecclesiastes 4:9–10 says, "Two are better than one, because they have a good return for their labor: if either of them falls down, one can help the other up. But pity anyone who falls and has no one to help them up." Counseling may be the support you need. If God is directing you to take those steps, ensure your counselor also shares your faith.

YOUR PRAYER LIFE

How are you approaching God? Boldly or with meekness? Are you fearful of Him or do you have faith that He's listening when you speak to Him? When you confide in the Holy Spirit, are you mindful to listen too? Do you wait for Him to speak or demand that He speak—according to your agenda? Do you trust Him to meet your needs, or do you doubt that He cares? God is your King. The Holy Spirit is your friend and Counselor. You can be assured that He cares about your needs, He will meet them, and He knows exactly how and when.

Being persistent in prayer is a vital habit and responsibility. Are you consistent in praying for your breakthrough? Consistency in prayer will build your faith in God and make you tenacious. "Then Jesus told his disciples . . . that they should always pray and not give up" (Luke 18:1). If you don't know what to pray for, the Bible reassures us that the Holy Spirit will pray on our behalf: "In the same way, the Spirit helps us in our weakness. We do not know what we ought to pray for, but the Spirit himself prays for us. He prays through groans too deep for words" (Romans 8:26 ESV). Prayer is our lifeline and privilege. Some breakthroughs in forgiveness and emotional healing are only made possible through a combination of prayer and fasting.

> But Jesus took him by the hand and lifted him up, and he arose. And when He had come into the house, His disciples asked Him privately, "Why could we not cast it out?" So He said to them, "This kind can come out by nothing but prayer and fasting." (Mark 9:27–29 NKJV)

FASTING

Fasting can be used to help break the stronghold of unforgiveness and emotional dysfunction. Together, prayer and fasting positions our hearts and minds to gain better spiritual clarity, discernment, answers from God, and guidance, among other things. Fasting is designated as a specific amount of time to draw closer to God while denying ourselves gratification from food and focusing our attention instead on Him through increased prayer and study of His Word. Fasting sharpens our spiritual perspectives as we believe and wait on God to answer our petitions.

Some choose to forgo meals all day, or during a specific time of the day. As with anything, please use wisdom when it comes to fasting. Consult God and your physician, especially if medications are a part of your daily regimen. If God is leading you to incorporate fasting, you should seek out the proper medical guidance on what to do and how fasting will best suit you.

God understands and cares deeply about your feelings. He cares about the wrong that has occurred in your life. He cares so much that he will not allow you to remain in the pain of offense and dwell aimlessly in the past. He doesn't want you to be a slave anymore.

Forgiveness and healing are not for those who are lazy. You will have to battle for it, and you'll have to fight to maintain a forgiving heart. It is a lifestyle. But you don't have to fight alone. Look into the eyes of Jesus and take His hand. Take the hand of the One who's asking you, *Do you want to be made whole?* He has given you everything you need to fight. Believe in His Word and take a stand.

Miracles happen when you consume the Word of God. When you make it the first and final authority of your life, you cannot help but change for the better. Digest it. Meditate on it. Follow it. Write it down. Apply and believe it.

Getting to the other side of forgiveness requires your participation, not your stagnation. Participate. Show up, even when you want to give in. Press into Jesus, and He will give you His supernatural strength and power to cross over to the other side.

The Forgiving Tip #2

Forgiveness is a decision, not a feeling. When you transform your mind, you elevate your life. Get up and walk!

Reflection Scripture

No, dear brothers and sisters, I have not achieved it, but I focus on this one thing: Forgetting the past and looking forward to what lies ahead, I press on to reach the end of the race and receive the heavenly prize for which God, through Christ Jesus, is calling us.
Philippians 3:13-14 NLT

❧ Take A Moment ❧

Reflect:

1) The excuses I've used are:

2) My system(s) of support are:

3) I can fully commit to turning the page by:

Act

- Make a list of what's holding you back and why.
- Create goals and an action plan for your mental and emotional health. You can break these goals down into prayer, thoughts, behavior, counseling, etc., or whatever you believe is conducive to your dilemma. Where do you see yourself in six months or one year from now? How do you plan to get there?

Prayer

Heavenly Father,

I admit I've made a lot of excuses as to why I can't forgive. My hurt, disappointment, and anger have become so comfortable that I've made them a part of my life. But today, I want more. I choose to own what I can control. I choose to stop making excuses and turn the page. I want to be whole, and today—this very minute—I am deciding to accept what You have to offer. Forgive me for rejecting You and making excuses. Forgive me for refusing the healing that has been available to me all along. You said in Your Word that you came so that I might have life, and have it more abundantly. Lord, I want the abundant life that You have already set for me. Lord, I no longer want my past to rob me of my present and future. Help me always choose You. And by choosing You, I desire the abundant life that does not include withholding forgiveness. I give You my pain and accept Your healing balm in exchange. I no longer wait for anyone else to stir the waters of healing. You are my Great Physician, and Your Word says that You bind up the brokenhearted. I give You all my wounds, and I'm prepared to do the work. Thank You for seeing about me.

In Jesus's name,

Amen

chapter 3

Get to the Root

It was pride that changed angels into devils, it is humility that makes men as angels.

~Saint Augustine

WE HAVE AN enemy. The world may not see him as a threat or acknowledge his existence, but he's here and has been for a long time. Like a detective, he's followed and studied you with a keen eye. Watching your every move—what you say and how you say it. Studying your likes and dislikes so that he can use them against you. He's an expert at planting seeds of deception and unstable thoughts. He's hoping you produce behavior and speech that goes against God. When he knows you're a believer, you become a threat and a target. You're his opposition, and he will fight you every step of the way by attempting to stop, silence, or discourage you. And when you're trying to grow and redeem your past, you will make him angry. If you know the truth about him, God, and who you are in Christ, he knows you will become a powerful force to be reckoned with.

That's his fear. So, he tries to throw you off course and prevent you from becoming all that you're meant to be—all that God wants you to be. He doesn't come showing off all his cards and tricks. Nor does he show up with telltale horns that would immediately reveal his identity. He comes in subtle ways that are easily overlooked if you're searching for the obvious. But he's scheming, along with his followers, about ways to take you out—morally, emotionally, physically, and spiritually. You see, that's his ultimate goal, and he's no rookie. With a calculated plan, he's after the heart and worship of everyone—especially Christians.

He's after you and won't let up.

With every chance he can get, he's intent on capturing your attention through devious means. Your strengths and weaknesses are tools that he will use against you. He delights in deception that appears innocent and kind rather than grandiose.

He first appeared on earth as a serpent, deceiving Eve in the Garden by whispering questions that would send her mind in dangerous directions and planting seeds of doubt. From Eve's perspective, what he said made a lot of sense. Adam and Eve walked with God and were able to feast off all of the trees in the Garden . . . except for one. They had explicit instructions of what to do and what not to do, and they obeyed accordingly—until the day the serpent planted seeds of uncertainty in Eve's mind and changed the course of humanity.

The more the serpent caused Eve to wonder about all she and Adam *could not* have, the more vulnerable she became to his influence. It didn't take long before he had her right where he wanted her. At that moment, she began to reassess God's instructions. Adam and Eve ultimately took the bait the serpent offered and chose disobedience. Through Eve, the serpent caused Adam, her husband, to take his eyes off God and sin.

> The serpent was the shrewdest of all the wild animals the LORD God had made. One day he asked the woman, "Did God really say you must not eat from the trees in the garden?" "Of course we may eat fruit from the trees in the garden," the woman replied. "It's only the fruit from the tree in the middle of the garden that we are not allowed to eat. God said, you must not eat it or even touch it' if you do, you will die." "You won't die!" the serpent replied to the woman. "God knows that your eyes will be opened as soon as you eat it, and you will be like God, knowing both good and evil." The woman was convinced.... So she took some of the fruit and ate it. Then she gave some to her husband, who was with her, and he ate it too. (Genesis 3:1–6 NLT)

If you want to know why you think you can't forgive, you need to look no further.

Many do not understand and recognize how unforgiveness is a ploy concocted by the one whose primary goal is to set you up to fail. He is the ultimate master orchestrator and manipulator behind the offense plaguing you and your inability to rise above it. Likewise, many fail to see how the enemy will use this means of entry to keep you bound in the past and imprisoned by unforgiveness. When you focus so much on what happened yesterday and your feelings attached to those events, you unwittingly become a willing participant in his subversive plan. Your offense may have come from others, but your inability to forgive can be attributed to the devil and his fallen angels. He is the puppet master working behind the scenes.

Like a big production, the stage is set for your downfall—but only if you fall for it. At first glance, all may look well, but a lot is going on spiritually that isn't immediately apparent.

SPIRITUAL WARFARE and STRONGHOLDS

For our struggle is not against flesh and blood, but against the rulers, against the authorities, against the powers of this dark world and against the spiritual forces of evil in the heavenly realms.
Ephesians 6:12

Before a spiritual attack can be dismantled, you must know exactly who's behind it, his tactics, and the preventative measures that will stop further damage from occurring. In the book of Genesis, we meet the enemy in the form of a serpent, but his story doesn't start there. His initial fall from grace is a stark reminder of what God condemns and the consequences of disobedience.

> "How you are fallen from heaven, O shining star, son of the morning! You have been thrown down to the earth, you who destroyed the nations of the world. For you said to yourself, 'I will ascend to heaven and set my throne above God's stars. I will preside on the mountain of the gods far away in the north. I will climb to the highest heavens and be like the Most High.'" (Isaiah 14:12–14 NLT)

The enemy began his existence as an angelic creation of God. His name was Lucifer, and he was also referred to as "morning/shining star." He was known as beautiful and wise, not only to others but also to himself. He was so impressed by himself, in fact, that he wanted to exalt himself above God. He wanted others to follow him and desired to be like God. The consequences of his rebellion included judgment and expulsion from heaven. He was cast "into the eternal fire prepared for the devil and his demons" (Matthew 25:41 NLT). He was also stripped of his old name and given a new one—Satan, which means "adversary."

Satan missed the memo that God competes with no one. Angels created by God will never be like God. Lucifer was given his walking papers and exiled to the place where he will spend eternity—hell. God is serious about sin and takes no delight in punishing anyone. An adversary of God is certainly not a friend of God. An adversary is an enemy—one who makes a conscious decision to reject God and what He stands for.

Pride is why Lucifer fell, and pride is what the enemy uses to tempt and keep you imprisoned by the past and bound by unforgiveness.

Pride is self-centered, always turning inward, and loves to exalt itself.

Pride says, *I can't move past this offense.*

Pride screams, *They don't deserve my forgiveness!*

Pride reminds you of your past.

Pride shames you and causes you to live in regret.

Pride says my wounds are too hurtful to be healed.

Pride sends constant reminders of what they did, when they did it, and how it came to be.

Pride doesn't take a day off.

Pride needs you to partner with pain and come into agreement for it to be effective.

Pride comes from the father of lies, the one who fell because of pride and the one who still lives in pride. Recognize that Satan is always prideful and that right now, he's using your hurt, pain, and offense as a weapon against you. Your offense has taken up residency and is ultimately rooted in pride.

The great news is that you can evict your offense by taming your pride.

Make no mistake about it, pride can be subtle and woven into aspects of truth. However, truth does not lie within the enemy, and many find themselves deceived by his "half-truths." Satan used pride to tempt Jesus in the wilderness to forfeit His purpose and destiny (see Matthew 4:1-11). Surely he utilizes the same scheme to trip you up as well. No matter how tough you may seem on the outside, unforgiveness and wounding make you vulnerable.

God deserves your worship, but Satan seeks to steal it away. If God is not a priority in your life, things, people, or the enemy become your focal points of worship. By holding on to your pain and the ones who've hurt you, unforgiveness *becomes* your God. **When you choose to withhold a nagging offense from God, you inadvertently partner with the enemy. Inevitably you are electing to believe that your emotions and offense have more power than God. That, my friend, is pride.**

And that's what Satan wants. The enemy desires for you to keep looking back at your past and staring at your old wounds. He longs for you to continue saying, "Look at what happened to me." I know your intention is not to place offense on a pedestal, but when you exalt what occurred above God, that's a win for the enemy.

I wasn't aware of this truth until the Holy Spirit illuminated it in my life. Yes, it's a hard pill to swallow, but the reality is, in the long run, it's more difficult to continue believing that unforgiveness, and all that comes with it, has less to do with you and more to do with what happened *to* you.

Pride opposes all that God stands for. Pride is selfish. It tempts you to focus on yourself when God says, "Focus on me." It has no room for God and no place in the kingdom of God. Pride prompts you to hold on to unforgiveness and turn inward instead of looking up to the One who can rescue you. Doesn't it make sense that the enemy would be so crafty as to tempt you with the sin that caused his own undoing?

If you didn't know, the enemy is consistent and specific in the weapons and approaches he uses to paralyze your Christian walk. The enemy was banished from heaven because he wanted to be like God, and when Adam and Eve experienced temptation in the Garden, the serpent suggested they could be like God. Pride was the source of it all, and pride continues to be the root cause of the disease called unforgiveness. It is the job of the enemy to make Christians ineffective in their ability to thrive and be productive. Pride is the number one means of keeping you imprisoned in your past, and it will take more than just you to defeat it. The enemy has a plan to harm you: spiritually, mentally, and, yes, physically. The enemy wants to:

Kill your faith.

Steal your inheritance.

Destroy your relationship with God and other people.

Those are his ultimate goals, as spelled out in John 10:10: "The thief only comes to kill and steal and destroy." The enemy delights in replaying mental images and words associated with your offense. He's intent on causing you to believe this hurt is more significant than God. He wants you to be guarded with paralyzing fear—to the point of weakening your ability to love and maintain healthy relationships. Satan doesn't want you to have peace. Rather, he wants you to wrestle with the pain and worry that plagues you. He doesn't want you to see a way out. He desires to keep you from the blessings God has for you and hinder you from thriving in your present. He wants to infiltrate your life so much so that others will be impacted negatively by your hurt and unbelief. And yes, he would love for you to stay bound forever.

But God has a plan, and the enemy knows it.

Satan is aware that his days are numbered. Although the eternal battle has already been won, take the initiative to keep fighting today. To guard yourself against the lies and tactics of the enemy. "Be alert and of sober mind. Your enemy the devil prowls around like a roaring lion looking for someone to devour" (1 Peter 5:8).

How do you get prepared? By arming yourself with the right tools, starting with the Word of God. Being casual with the enemy is not the answer. He knows what the Bible says and has studied your ways. If you want to get to the other side, you must research and be aware of his schemes.

> Finally, be strong in the Lord and in his mighty power. Put on the full armor of God, so that you can take your stand against the devil's schemes.... Stand firm then, with the belt of truth buckled around your waist, with the breastplate of righteousness in place, and with your feet fitted with readiness that comes from the gospel of peace. In addition to this, take up the shield of faith, with which you can extinguish all the flaming arrows of the evil one. Take the

helmet of salvation and the sword of the Spirit, which is the word of God. And pray in the Spirit on all occasions with all kinds of prayers and requests. With this in mind, be alert and always keep on praying for all the Lord's people. (Ephesians 6:10–11, 13–18)

By not allowing pride to have its way, we can defeat the enemy and dismantle his tactics. Make no mistake about it; he will try to stop you at all costs. Moving past unforgiveness will be challenging because you're spiritually up against an adversary who is strategizing your demise—and using unforgiveness as one of the means to do it.

Refuse to go one more day being oppressed, tormented, and deceived by him. God has power over all. Because you have Him, you can overcome. As the Word says, you are "more than conquerors"! (Romans 8:37).

The enemy wants you to get stuck in the sins of pride and unforgiveness and remain in the stench of your past. He desires that you take your eyes off the One—God—who makes all things new. If the enemy can keep you rooted in pride, you'll miss the lesson, stunt your spiritual growth, and, yes, even miss out on blessings.

Pride is a weed that can be uprooted and a hurt that can be healed. Your ego that's rooted in unforgiveness can be transformed into purpose. Saying yes to God's will and releasing your offender will place your heart in the right position to intentionally keep pride out.

The Forgiving Tip #3

When you locate its root, you have the power to eradicate and dismantle the fruit of unforgiveness.

Reflection Scripture

Humble yourselves before the Lord, and he will lift you up in honor.
James 4:10 NLT

❦ Take A Moment ❦

Reflect

1) I realize that pride has shown up through:
2) The enemy has deceived me by:

Action Plan

- Acknowledge you have an enemy who wants nothing but destruction for your life, and keeping you in unforgiveness is one of his tactics.
- Study your enemy by getting into the Word of God. Most of all, get introduced to, reacquainted with, and grow deeper in Jesus Christ. When you access Him, you access His power.

Prayer

Heavenly Father,

I didn't know the seriousness of holding on to unforgiveness. What they did hurt so much, but I had no idea that pride was at the root of my stagnancy and unwillingness to let go of the thing causing me offense. Forgive me for treating unforgiveness like an idol. Forgive me for unknowingly partnering with the enemy, whose job it is to take me out by any means necessary. Now that You've made me aware, help me release and reconcile the past. Help me tear down my spirit of pride and replace it with humility. Lord, I acknowledge that pride has robbed me of peace and a right relationship with You. Therefore, I need your wisdom, and desire to accept the peace You want to give. Help me choose humility instead of offense. Teach me to hate pride and anything that's not like You. You are perfect, kind, and true. Thank You for this gift of revelation that can transform my life. Thank You for not only healing my symptoms but also helping me discover their source as well. I declare that I will forgive and heal.

In Jesus's name,

Amen

chapter 4

When Your Expectations are Shattered

Bitterness believes the lie that nothing good can come out of the hand you've been dealt.

LIFE CAN CERTAINLY be unscripted. We plan and we hope. We believe that good things are waiting around the corner. And sometimes they are. However, despite all our preparation and the preventive measures we take, some chapters in our lives may deal us a bad hand. When life shows up in ways you don't anticipate, what do you do?

In the book of Ruth, we meet Naomi, who shows us how life's storms can arrive suddenly and leave behind a trail of debris and disappointing circumstances that brings us to our knees. Death had already taken her husband, and now it had stolen her sons too. The boys she raised and watched grow into fine young men were now gone. Naomi's heart was wrought with pain and unanswered questions. Who would take care of her? Who would protect and love her? The hand that life had dealt her seemed cruel. What did she do to deserve this? No husband, sons, or grandchildren. The future Naomi had always dreamt about now seemed bleak. Life, she thought, had treated her unfairly and left her heart broken in pieces.

Losing the one she loved had been hard. Her protector and provider. A faithful husband who kept her life secure and future certain. With him, she had tasted the goodness of life. Without him, she experienced sadness and a void that only he could fill. Although her children could not replace her longing for intimate love from a husband, their love and presence reminded Naomi that life could go on somehow. At least they were able to understand her sorrow and grieve with her. And she did move forward, with all of the courage she could muster. Life didn't stop. As her sons went on to marry, Naomi looked forward to having grandchildren. She thought surely they would add to her life, filling her up with joy.

It took much strength for Naomi to carry on after the death of her husband. But the death of her sons was her tipping point. We've all had our moments where enough is enough, and no parent ever expects to lose their child. Grief, hurt, and confusion replaced the joy she once had.

With her future uncertain, Naomi sought to go back to her homeland of Bethlehem. At least there she would be around family again, now that her own was no more. When her daughter-in-law Ruth, offered to accompany her, Naomi tried to turn her away for their own sake. Naomi didn't want Ruth to blindly follow her to this new land where she wouldn't be able to support herself. After all, she was young, beautiful, and eligible to remarry. She told Ruth, "Things are far more bitter for me than for you, because the Lord himself has raised his fist against me" (Ruth 1:13 NLT).

Naomi was blunt about the disappointment she felt after losing both her sons at the same time. As she and her daughters-in-law wept, Orpah decided to return to her parents' home as Naomi suggested. It was Ruth who stayed, as she could not imagine leaving Naomi, whom she loved. She expressed her devotion by saying:

> "Don't ask me to leave you and turn back. Wherever you go, I will go; wherever you live, I will live. Your people will be my people, and your God will be my God. Wherever you die, I will die and there I will be buried. May the LORD punish me severely if I allow anything but death to separate us!" When Naomi saw that Ruth was determined to go with her, she said nothing more. (Ruth 1:16–18 NLT)

As Naomi and Ruth arrived in Bethlehem, the town's women were excited to see a familiar face they had not seen in years, and they asked, "Is it really Naomi?" (Ruth 1:19 NLT). Naomi's response clearly communicates that her disappointment and sorrow had spiraled into pity and anger. As Naomi thought about all that had occurred, she spoke from the depths of her pain and bitter perspective on life:

> "Don't call me Naomi," she responded. "Instead, call me Mara, for the Almighty has made life very bitter for me. I went away full, but the LORD has brought me home empty. Why call me Naomi when the LORD has caused me to suffer and the Almighty has sent such tragedy upon me?" (Ruth 1:20–21 NLT)

We can all identify with Naomi's bitter attitude. Naomi didn't physically shake her fist at God, but she definitely blamed Him for what happened and for the grief she was going through. Her anger toward God caused bitterness to manifest and have a seat at the throne of her heart.

What hand has God dealt to *you* that is causing bitterness to rule and unforgiveness to reign in your life?

We've all been there.

We've all been afraid to say what God already knows: that we're offended by what God has done or did not do in our life. Do any of these scenarios sound familiar?

- Like Naomi, you're struggling to come to terms with the death of a loved one. Maybe you prayed and believed in their earthly healing, yet God decided to take them home to heaven. Maybe suicide has taken the one you love.

When Your Expectations Are Shattered

- Your life has been turned upside down because of a loved one's medical diagnosis.
- You hoped and believed for a restored marriage, but your spouse's rejection has landed you in divorce court.
- You find yourself in financial ruin because of a failed business venture you believed God had blessed.
- Your child, who was brought up in the church and a loving home, has decided that kind of life was your dream, not theirs.
- You believed that children would come soon after saying "I do," but you've struggled with fertility issues.
- You've waited a long time for God's chosen spouse to arrive, and you find yourself still waiting.
- You've lost your home and belongings to a natural disaster, and you wonder how anything good could come from it.

Yes, life doesn't discriminate. For some, the cycle of tragedy can seem never-ending. When things fall apart, you're left feeling shocked and blindsided, standing in awe of the shattered pieces of your life. When your plans and expectations don't come to fruition, disappointment sets in.

That's what happened to Naomi. She was plagued by thoughts of *How did this happen... again?* and *Why did this happen... now?* Wife and mother, now mourner. The dark clouds of her life seemed to cover any glimmers of hope. She became closely acquainted with mourning and pain. For Naomi, all hope was gone when the ones she loved died. Maybe, like Naomi, hope has left you too. She knew God, but that knowing wasn't enough to save her loved ones' lives. That's why she was convinced her ending had come, but little did she know that God had a new beginning for her on the other side.

When things happen in ways you don't like or did not expect, or when circumstances appear contrary to God's goodness, we fall into "the blame game." Perhaps God has allowed your season of suffering, and in the midst of your weariness, unbelief, and pain, you find yourself building a case against Him. You fall into the trap of believing that the Author of life dealt you a bad hand. Season after season, continuous trials and bad news keep mounting. You may wonder, *Could anything else go wrong?*

And just when you think life couldn't get any worse, it does. Instead of saying, "Life has let me down," you really want to say, "*God* has let me down. He allowed it and He did it." **Perhaps you've already said it, and I understand if you have.**

Naomi suffered immense loss and had every right to grieve the deaths of her family members. Her expectations of growing old with her husband were gone. Her desire to see her sons become fathers vanished as well. The grim reality of Naomi's life didn't come close to anything she had imagined for herself. And because life had failed her, because she believed God had given her a bad hand, Naomi's heart no longer carried any joy or expectation of good. Her sadness gave way to anger that turned inward, producing the right conditions for bitterness to take root. Before she knew it, Naomi became the walking billboard for bitterness. Her inability to make peace with the hand she'd been dealt kept her from seeing the new hand of blessings that waited on the other side of her grief.

What about you? Are you having a hard time seeing past your grief and loss? Has your hope faded because of circumstances outside your control?

You have every right to grieve. For loved ones killed by violence. For those who died from sickness. For those whom God chose to receive their healing in heaven. For the dream that died. For the relationship that failed, and the opportunity that slipped from your grasp. Yes, your grief, loss, and pain are real, and I grieve with you. But while grief has no specific time frame, consider that maybe your mourning has gotten in the way of your living.

Grief can be complicated and mean different things to different people. It can look different for everyone. Taking on different shapes over time and resurfacing sporadically. Showing up without an appointment and not being triggered by anything. I'm not here to tell you to "get over it." Yes, you have every right to grieve. But, if you decide to throw in the towel on hope and let your bitterness take up permanent residence, you'll forfeit the awesome future God has in store for you.

There's no way around it; whenever we begin to place limits on God and expect Him to work according to our timing and priorities, disappointment is guaranteed.

Again, you have every right to grieve. But you can't stay there. That's not what you want.

Memories have a heartbeat and life of their own. Rehearsing what happened and what didn't happen, from the same place of pain and disappointment, keeps memories alive. How many bad memories are you keeping alive?

Naomi's story teaches us that we have to fight for our future and for our breakthroughs. You have to fight to get to the other side—past your grief, loss, and disappointments. But you don't have to fight alone. If you have Jesus, you have hope. Even during times of loss, pain, and unmet expectations.

God works in ways *we* cannot see. While the enemy wants you to focus on smoke and mirrors, tempting you to believe that life and joy are no more, God has a plan already at work. I think our job lies not in trying to see the plan, but rather, in *believing* the *One* who has a plan. When you believe, you have hope!

God sees our beginning, middle, and end, and he wasn't taken by surprise at what happened to you. Or your response to it. As much as Naomi's pain clouded her view of the future, an awesome plan was unfolding as she placed one foot in front of the other.

The life experiences Naomi endured seemed unfair to her, but God was there as it all unfolded.

And He's there with you as well.

The enemy tried to disrupt God's plan by tricking Naomi into focusing on her bitterness toward God. Likewise, he tries to use the same tactic to derail God's plan for you. But the enemy lost with Naomi, and he will lose with you too. Grieving your loss while still maintaining hope *is* possible. Do not let bitterness settle in the depths of your heart.

If it's there, you have access to the power of God to snatch. It. Out.

How? Against all hope, Abraham in hope believed and so became the father of many nations, just as it had been said to him, "So shall your offspring be." (Romans 4:18)

Against all hope, Abraham believed.

Against all hope.

Against *all* hope.

Believe God in the unseen.

Believe God *for* the unseen.

Believe *God*.

When you believe God, bitterness cannot take up residence, and hope will spring forth!

The Forgiving Tip #4

When you let disappointment and grief become your god, you leave no room for God to work.

Reflection Scripture

The LORD is close to the brokenhearted and saves those who are crushed in spirit.
Psalm 34:18

✽ Take A Moment ✽

Reflect

1.) I'm disappointed at God because:

2.) I've allowed bitterness to impact me by:

Act

- Focus on what's going right in your life. Identify three things you're grateful for.

- Write a letter to God explaining your disappointment, and then write Him a letter that focuses on how you believe He can help you overcome the disappointment you've faced.

Prayer

Dear Lord,

I've been disappointed and bitter about how life has turned out for me. I never expected to be going through this. I feel as though You've forsaken me and dealt me the wrong hand. Because of this, I've allowed my bitterness to shift my focus away from You. Please forgive me for falsely believing that You're uncaring and that my circumstances have more power over my life than You. Forgive me for resorting to self- pity and despair. Forgive me for renaming myself "bitter" rather than honoring the name You gave me at birth: "blessed." Lord, I have no idea what the future holds, and I'm scared of the unknown. Help me see Your hand in the present, preparing a better future for me. Because You already know what's in store, help me trust in You as I shake off unforgiveness. Lastly, help me be at peace and content with the life You have carefully fashioned for me, even though some parts I'd rather do without. Help me embrace the process as You make me more like You by using the suffering in my life. I declare today that disappointment, bitterness, and unforgiveness no longer reside in me. As I look forward to the future with hope and anticipation, Lord, help me believe in You . . . against all hope!

Amen

chapter 5

When You've Been Dropped

Apologies are nice, but it's not a requirement for you to forgive.

SOME SCARS STAY with you for life. They serve as a constant reminder of what occurred because of your own choices or those of others. At times they happen to the most vulnerable: the young, poor, or those who don't have the knowledge or resources to change their circumstances. Mephibosheth was five when it happened to him. As a child who grew up with more opportunities than his peers but who ultimately became a crippled, ostracized adult, he knew how one unfortunate incident could change the trajectory of a person's life. However, that did not keep him from being remembered by the One who had the power to right the wrong done to him.

As the son of Johnathan, King Saul's eldest son, Mephibosheth had no reason to suspect there was impending danger lurking in his future. But as a young boy, full of life and vigor, he became the victim of a split-second decision. Upon hearing the news that his father Johnathan was killed, Mephibosheth's nurse panicked. As someone who had cared for him all his life, she tried to save him from harm and those who might threaten his life as well. But in panic and haste, she dropped him.

> Saul's son Johnathan had a son named Mephibosheth, who was crippled as a child. He was five years old when the report came from Jezreel that Saul and Johnathan had been killed in battle. When the child's nurse heard the news, she picked him up and fled. But as she hurried away, she dropped him, and he became crippled. (2 Samuel 4:4 NLT)

Unfortunately, her best intentions proved to be detrimental. The incident left him with a permanent injury. Her last-minute reaction to devastating family news changed him from the grandson of a king to an outcast. From then on, he had to grow accustomed to a life of physical and social limitations.

In Hebrew, Mephibosheth means "the mouth of shame." And after being dropped, his life was full of shame. He had to endure the disgrace of his family's defeat, questions about the legacy of his lineage, and withstand the rejection of many who defined him by his limp and saw it as a nuisance.

Mephibosheth's experience is not an isolated one. Like him, we have all been shunned at some point in our lives. **You may not have been dropped physically, but the pain from rejection can leave you crippled with offense.**

REJECTION

According to Merriam-Webster, *rejection* is the refusal "to accept, submit to, take for some purpose, or use. To refuse to hear, receive, or admit. To cast off. To spew out." Rejection can certainly bring out feelings of insecurity, causing you to question who you are, what you know, and ultimately your worth. The enemy can have a field day using rejection to play with your emotions and make you feel like you're not good enough.

Rejection may not be as loud or noticeable as other offenses at the onset, but it's effective at highlighting half-truths about yourself and situations that involve you. The following examples are not an exhaustive list. However, they are extremely common and represent all the ways the offense of rejection can take hold in your life. These common scenarios serve as the enemy's bait. When you believe the lie, you begin to feed off it and internalize it, making you less than useful in your life and to those around you.

- When friends betray you.
- When promises are not kept.
- When he/she no longer loves you.
- When your spouse wants a divorce.

- When you're uninvited.
- When you're overlooked for the promotion.
- When your employer lets you go.
- When the church turns its back on you.

There's a common theme that connects all these different forms of rejection. And it's all too familiar: **Most often, rejection happens unexpectedly and is perpetrated by someone we know.**

Rejection can be damaging because it strikes at the core of who we are: our personality, looks, worldview, etc. When faced with rejection, we often turn inward and ask ourselves, *What parts of me were not likable or desirable? Why?* We attempt to analyze and make sense of our broken relationships in an effort to assign blame to someone or something. The process may leave us with unanswered questions, fear, and bitterness. When one's identity is attacked, we immediately assume that it's personal. We become offended by those who gave us a false sense of security, hope, or a temporary guarantee that we'd been chosen. Perhaps they walked with you for years, ate with you, and displayed loyalty at one time, and now you're faced with trying to understand their change of heart. This is exactly what the adversary wants. **He wants us to embrace the lie that what you have or who you are is not good enough or wanted.**

For some, the search for validation continues for a long time. For others, they recognize this divisive tactic of the enemy and shut it down. For everyone, rejection is a lesson that's either painful or purposeful—the choice is ours to make. From the outside, rejection looks personal. However, there's a greater purpose behind it. If you continue to focus on being dropped, you'll miss seeing and understanding God's purpose behind the heartache. **Rejection is God's protection and His plan for your new direction. And He's using this route to place the pieces of your puzzle together, perfectly.** Remember, Romans 8:28 tells us "that all things work together for good to them that love God, to them that are called according to His purpose."

The spirit of rejection is the cousin of offense. It can rob you of healthy future relationships and damage your current relationships. The spirit of rejection looks for ulterior motives when there may be none, believing lies that may not be there, and introducing you to paranoia and assumptions. Rejection can be deadly to your future because it minimizes the hope and good that's possible by tricking you into believing that personal connections only result in pain and disappointment.

The spirit of rejection causes you to become more sensitive to tone, behavior, and feelings. It may cause you to misinterpret your interactions with others and perceive conflicts that aren't real. The enemy is delighted when you allow rejection to keep you bound, confused, and questioning your identity, because you are more likely to believe his lies that God is not good and that you're not worthy of friends, love, or great opportunities. If you're unsure of who you are, you're at risk of forsaking the One who created you and knows you intimately.

Offense birthed from rejection usually happens over time as it sits in your mind and heart. Rejection grows and thrives on bitterness, confusion, and isolation. But you will never hear the enemy whisper this truth about rejection:

> **Rejection is what happened.**
> **But it is not who you are.**
> **You are Chosen and loved by the Creator—God.**
> **He will never reject those He calls His own.**

PERSONAL REGRET

Offense from rejection is also typical when apologies are absent. Unforgiveness coupled with rejection builds the false narrative that receiving closure is the only way to settle your heart, relieve your pain, and move forward. The enemy uses this tactic to keep painful memories of rejection alive by preying on your perceived need that getting closure from your offender is the cure.

And so you desire closure. You hope and wait to receive an apology for being overlooked. An apology for being rejected. An apology for being dropped intentionally, without explanation or second thought. And it just doesn't happen. Instead you discover that the individuals you once shared a relationship with are happy without your presence. Or they at least appear to be. Meanwhile, you sulk, cry, and overreact to everything and anyone standing before you. Yes, rejection hurts and can be unkind. You're left to pick up the pieces because of someone else's decision or mistake.

But keep in mind that Mephibosheth's injury was life-altering.

Yours doesn't have to be.

The pain of rejection has overwhelmed my life on numerous occasions. However, one story stands out from the rest.

We met during our senior year in high school. Through no choice of her own, she was forced into this new environment: New school, new faces, and new experiences. But our connection was instant. Despite our opposite personalities, a fast friendship was formed. Me, convincing her the glass is always half full, and her, persuading me that it was always half empty. We laughed and hung out as teenagers would. However, college eventually came into the picture. She left for school and I stayed home. We initially kept in touch, and I was thrilled to visit her one weekend at her school.

Over time, our diminishing communication became harder to ignore. Slowly but surely, the calls and catching up stopped. I understood she was in a different world and had every right to be excited about her new chapter in life. But when it became clear that she had moved on and fully immersed herself into her new life, I was not prepared. I had not anticipated engaging in a new season of friendships during my first year of college. While I understood that she'd make new friends, I always thought I'd remain her friend too, and I found myself saddened by her unexpected rejection.

As she turned the page on our friendship, I found it difficult to do so. After some time, I finally accepted the reality that I was no longer a part of her circle of friends. Instead, I felt as though our memories were attached to a high school that *she* never fully embraced. I went on with my life but still recalled great moments when our friendship gave me joy.

When I joined Facebook, I searched for her to try and reconnect. Occasionally, we would chat, and one day we mutually decided to meet up for Mexican food. I looked forward to seeing and catching up face-to-face. However, as our lunch date drew closer, an inward shift happened for me. I realize now that it had been there for quite some time. **When you do not deal with things that bother you, they will eventually resurface.**

I realized how angry and profusely hurt I was. I recalled the change in our friendship years ago and realized I'd been holding on to the offense for over five years.

"Time heals all wounds" means nothing when your time is not dedicated to healing those wounds. I had the time, yet my wounds were as present as ever. They sat and festered as I fed them past memories, the pain I felt, and all that I *wanted* to happen. I understand now that I desired an apology or explanation for what had occurred. I hoped for closure, which is all too common when friends begin new chapters in life. I allowed feelings of rejection to blind me, and two days before our meeting, I canceled.

Sending a message that I could not attend was my resolution. Yes, I was immature and still hurting. I didn't want to face the person who had taken the friendship that I deeply cherished for granted. From my perspective at the time, I could not meet the person who I believed rejected me, because I was ashamed. I feared to tell her the truth and was embarrassed that I, this Christian girl, had allowed a grudge to influence me and keep me from truly embracing the beauty of new relationships for so long.

If I knew then what I know now, I would have kept our lunch date.

Then one day, in the summer of 2015, I was scrolling through Facebook during my break at work. I noticed a new photo of my friend in my newsfeed. Then another. There were so many pictures of her flooding my feed that I went to her page to figure out what was going on. I could not believe my eyes. The announcement of her death stunned me.

She was gone.

How could this be? What happened? Questions began to flood my mind while I frantically searched for reasons why. Also, feelings of regret began to consume me immediately. *Why did I cancel our lunch?* I should have met her for our outing. I should have kept our date. She was gone, and I didn't get a chance to say goodbye.

She had passed away shortly before Memorial Day. To honor the burial customs of her African heritage, her funeral service would occur thirty to sixty days after her death. By divine providence, not only did I find out the same week of her scheduled memorial service, but God also provided me with a gift that I cherish to this day.

While driving to my counseling internship at a local elementary school and during the time I spent with students there, my friend continued to be at the forefront of my mind. I kept berating myself that I should have met with her when I had the chance and just gotten over our lack of communication. Thoughts of "what if" ran through my mind as I recounted our last words. Shock and regret enveloped me as I realized that I could not go back. She was gone.

This time I was sure that my words would not be heard. As I left my internship and headed back to work, God spoke to me in so many ways. Now I reflect with a smile as I recall how God provided me with comfort and confirmation on that day.

While listening to the radio, the topic of the program was forgiveness. Immediately I knew that God was using this program to get my attention, as it could not have come at a more perfect time. As I drove, I also noticed someone from my past who looked familiar. Sure enough, it was *another* friend that I'd lost touch with. It was another person I'd felt offended by. Without hesitation, I pulled over to say hello, and we embraced as though time had never passed between us.

As we spoke, any offense I'd held against her dropped instantly. I no longer cared about what did or did not happen. I only knew what I did not want to happen again. At that moment, I appreciated life more—and the people in my life. I knew that I did not want to spend any more time being held hostage by offense.

I didn't want to trade a friend or associate for a friendship with unforgiveness.

In one day, God comforted me, revealed my erroneous perspective, and provided a new beginning. God knew what I didn't know. He knew what was waiting around the corner and extended an opportunity for grace and comfort as events unraveled.

I could not speak to my friend who passed, but God provided me with an opportunity to learn a valuable lesson: At the end of the day, when a life has passed away—will your

grudge be that serious? Forgive today; the next moment is promised to no one.

When I think of forgiveness, this story of my late friend is among the top examples that come to mind. I grieved for her, for us, and what could have been. I'll never know if we would have rekindled our friendship, or if our meetup would have been two old friends catching up. But what happened is something I never want to happen again.

REDEEMING THE TIME

"Time heals all wounds." We hear those words, and though it sounds good, time by itself is not the answer. Many let time pass by and allow their hurt to evolve into anger, which can ultimately lead to bitterness and resentment. If this sounds familiar, the question to ask yourself is this: What are you doing with that time? Would you be so presumptuous to believe you have time left? Many who are wounded from rejection often prolong their healing because of the misconception that closure is needed. Just because you've moved on doesn't mean you've accepted and let go of your need for closure. It could be that your thoughts on closure go something like this:

> If only they would say *something* . . .
> I need them to own what they did . . .
> I want them to be sorry . . .
> They *should* be sorry for what they did to me . . .
> I could move on if they would apologize . . .

Apologies are nice, but are they needed for you to forgive, heal, and get on with your life?

Absolutely not.

I realize now that my offense from rejection also masked a desire to receive an apology. However, God revealed a new perspective to me on closure.

Before my friend died, I presumed getting closure would be the cure to my bitterness and pain. After you've experienced rejection, it's easy to become consumed by this false perception that closure is necessary. You rationalize that an explanation or apology will satisfy your unanswered questions. Most times, that couldn't be further from the truth. The answer to your rejection lies in acceptance.

Accepting that God is in control.

Accepting that to everything there is a season.

Accepting that people come and go.

When rejection happens, we may not know what's on the other side. But believe that there's another side, and it gets better.

Closure does not come from the one who offends you. Instead, closure and resolution should ultimately come from the One who has the power to do something about your situation. And His name is Jesus.

MOVING FORWARD

As painful as rejection can be, it teaches you to loosen your grip on anything that comes into your life. Whether it's a job, friends, new opportunities, etc.—these things are only temporary in the grand scheme of God's plan for your life. Just like seasons, things and people change. That's why it's important to not only be flexible in your dealings but also to set proper boundaries (rather than build walls) in your life. Most importantly, being dropped reinforces the fact that the only constant in life is Christ. He will never fail. And, dear friends, *He* will not drop you. *He* will not let you fall.

While I never expected to grieve my friend's death with so much guilt and sorrow, God continues to provide lessons and shared opportunities for me to act on what He's revealed. Though tragic and unsettling, I have not shared my story of rejection to frighten you. Rather, my intent is to reframe your view and perspective. The reality is that death can come suddenly, leaving you with unfinished business and no time for reconciliation. However, you can choose to address difficult conversations and bad feelings as they happen to mitigate your chances of experiencing a scenario like mine.

Despite the rejection he endured throughout his life, Mephibosheth's story does not end in despair and indignity. Yes, he was permanently disabled through no fault of his own, and the Bible doesn't indicate whether his childhood nurse ever returned to apologize. However, his injury did not stop him from being remembered by King David.

> Now David said, "Is there still anyone who is left of the House of Saul, that I may show him kindness for Johnathan's sake?" . . . "There is still a son of Jonathan who is lame in his feet." . . . When Mephibosheth the son of Jonathan, the son of Saul, had come to David, he fell on his face and prostrated himself . . . "Here is your servant." "Do not fear, for I will surely show you kindness for Jonathan your father's sake, and will restore to you all the land of Saul your grandfather; and you shall eat bread at my table continually." (2 Samuel 9:1, 3, 6–7 NKJV)

Mephibosheth's injury did not prevent him from receiving restoration. His nurse dropped him, but King David recalled what happened in the past and kept his promise to his best friend, Johnathan. Mephibosheth's story teaches us that God is not only aware of your rejection but also intent to do something about it.

They may reject you, but you will always be accepted in Christ. His opinion concerning you matters the most.
Forgive those who dropped you.
Forgive those who did not see you as Christ does.
Forgive those who could not see you as God does.
Forgive those who betrayed you.
Forgive those who pretended to be friends yet were not.

Forgive those who said their love was real but lied.

Forgive those who liked or loved you at one time but had a change of heart.

Forgive those who were careless with their words.

Forgive those who were insensitive with their actions.

Forgive those who did not have the courage to have hard conversations with you.

Forgive those who did what they knew best at the time.

Forgive those who were great people, but their season in your life came to an end.

Forgive them.

The Forgiving Tip #5

When you let your grudge become the deciding factor, you can miss the redeeming work that God wants to do.

Reflection Scripture

"Can a mother forget the baby at her breast and have no compassion on the child she has borne? Though she may forget, I will not forget you!"

Isaiah 49:15

❧ Take A Moment ❧

Reflect:
1. I feel rejected when:
2. I can transform my view of rejection into acceptance from Christ by:

Act:
- List the great characteristics you have and what you bring to your relationships.
- Meditate and make a list on what Christ has said and feels about you. Then, continue to believe it.

Prayer

Dear Lord,

When I think about it, the rejection of others has hurt me to my core. I didn't realize the magnitude of my pain and the depth of my unforgiveness until now. Thank You for revealing the truth behind the mask I show to others. I thought receiving closure from them would heal me and help me forgive. Now I understand and know the truth. Help me view rejection from Your perspective. Help me see my role and their role in the story of my life. I admit that I still may not understand why it happened. However, I know that as I continue to trust in you, my faith will be strengthened. Please continue to draw me closer to You and increase my knowledge of just how much You love me. Father, I need You to wrap Your loving arms around me and heal every single part that feels rejected and has believed the lie of not being good enough. Please help me take those lies captive and reject them! Lord, I know that You will never drop or reject me. You said in Your Word that you would never leave or forsake me. Help me accept what you've already called me to be: Your child, loved, and an heir to the throne. I don't want to reject Your transformative power or reject what You've already given to me. Most of all, help me transform the misery that I've experienced and birth an incredible revelation of ministry. I know that in You nothing is wasted. Thank You for giving me beauty for ashes in the midst of my hurt and confusion.

Amen

chapter 6

When the Hurt is Close

"You intended to harm me, but God intended it all for good."

~Genesis 50:20 NLT

JOSEPH COULD NEVER have fathomed the path God had in store for him. As most do, at a ripe old age he began to reflect on just how far God had brought him. He was led to this place. Not by choice, but destiny. When Joseph recalled his formative years and his current position as the second-most powerful man in Egypt, he could only smile and marvel at what God had done. His journey had been long and hard, filled with triumphs and disappointments. It was a road *he* would not have chosen for himself. But through it all, God kept him and made good on His promise to bestow him with greatness and prosperity. Over time, God transformed his heart. Tears of sorrow were replaced by tears of joy until Joseph no longer questioned or held a grudge concerning the things that had happened to him in the past. Joseph came to understand that his family members were not his enemies. Instead, they were instruments in God's plan to grow and change him and save the lives of many. God brought Joseph to Egypt for a divine purpose. Although the detours along the way were unscripted and messy, the fulfillment of God's outcome was divine.

FAMILY MATTERS

Family. You did not choose them, but you were not placed among them by chance. Because God is sovereign, your familial placement was no mistake. It was strategic. No matter how confusing, hurtful, and disappointing your past was or current situation is, your position is purposeful. I understand that statement sparks many questions, but stay with me. As Christians, we do not operate by luck or chance. Our lives are not an afterthought to God. Psalm 37:23 (NKJV) tells us, "The steps of a good man are ordered by the LORD, and He delights in His way." We serve a big God who has intimately designed our lives and ordered our steps. In His will, He has assigned you to be a member of the family He chose for you. In His sovereignty, He can use the wrong done against you to elevate and accomplish the very purpose He has in mind.

Our first teachers in life to show us right from wrong, good and bad, are family members. They may introduce us to the complexities of relationships and life experiences, but sometimes the very ones destined to connect to us in this intimate familial way are also the ones who cause us the most pain—causing us to rethink our definitions of *enemy, jealousy,* and *love.* Families are supposed to be a fan club like no other. The ones you can depend on when all else fails, and a guiding light when life is difficult to understand.

But families are flawed. Filled with people who are trying to make sense of their *own* lives and feelings, sometimes hurting themselves and others along the way. If you didn't know by now, it's almost inevitable that members of your family will hurt you in one way or another. It may be unintentional or calculated. It may have everything to do with you—or nothing at all. I'm not sure what *your* story is, but acknowledging that all relationships will disappoint in some way may help you view your family through a different lens and maintain a reasonable perspective.

As we take a closer look at Joseph's story, we see that no family is exempt from drama and pain. Most of all, his story demonstrates the power of forgiveness when those closest to you hate you and attempt to set you up to fail.

STORY OF JOSEPH

If anyone can understand from experience that family will fail you, it's Joseph. His story begins at the age of seventeen. However, we can infer that family drama and conflict with Joseph started before his teenage years. Out of his eleven brothers, Joseph was his father, Jacob's, clear favorite. The Bible points out that Joseph would report back to his father about all the bad things his brothers were doing. Yes, Joseph was a tattletale—which only added fuel to an already volatile relationship with his siblings. To make things worse, Jacob gifted Joseph with a beautiful coat—a not-so-subtle gesture of his favor toward him.

> Jacob loved Joseph more than any of his other children because Joseph had been born to him in his old age. So one day Jacob had a special gift made for Joseph—a beautiful robe. But his brothers hated Joseph because their father loved him more than the rest of them. They couldn't say a kind word to him. (Genesis 37:3–4 NLT)

The Bible also indicates that Joseph bragged about his future greatness, which God had revealed to him in dreams. His inability to keep quiet and withhold the signs God had given him concerning his life also irked his brothers.

> One night Joseph had a dream, and when he told his brothers about it, they hated him more than ever. "Listen to this dream," he said. "We were out in the field, tying up bundles of grain. Suddenly my bundle stood up, and your bundles all gathered around and bowed low before mine!" His brothers responded, "So you think you will be our king, do you? Do you actually think you will reign over us?" And they hated him all the more because of his dreams and the way he talked about them. (Genesis 37:8 NLT)

Can you imagine the tension in the room? It appears everyone could sense it except for Joseph. He was either oblivious to the hatred and jealousy, or it just did not concern him. Nevertheless, Joseph—also known as "the dreamer"—had yet another revelation from God. This time, he told his brothers *and* father about it (see Genesis 37:9–11). Repeated dreams from God confirmed that Joseph would, in fact, hold a future leadership position.

God called Joseph to leadership at a young age. However, God did not reveal how he would gain a leadership role. Joseph's road to Egypt's royal courts was messy, but it was no mistake. His journey was filled with emotional pain, wrongful accusations, and several years in prison—all thanks to his brothers.

> When Joseph's brothers saw him coming, they recognized him in the distance. As he approached, they made plans to kill him. "Here comes the dreamer!" they said. Come on let's kill him and throw him into one of these cisterns. We can tell our father,' A wild animal has eaten him.' Then we'll see what becomes of his dreams!" (Genesis 37:18–20 NLT)

Their original plot had been to kill Joseph, but one brother suggested a less sinister idea, hoping to rescue Joseph at a later time. However, while the brothers agreed to throw him into an empty cistern, Joseph was ultimately sold into slavery.

But when Reuben heard of their scheme, he came to Joseph's rescue. "Let's not kill him," he said. "Why should we shed any blood? Let's just throw him into this empty cistern here in the wilderness. Then he'll die without our laying a hand on him." Reuben was secretly planning to rescue Joseph and return him to his father. (Genesis 37:21–22 NLT)

Judah said to his brothers, "What will we gain by killing our brother? His blood would just give us a guilty conscience. Instead of hurting him, let's sell him to those Ishmaelite traders. After all, he is our brother—our own flesh and blood!" . . . Some time later, Reuben returned to get Joseph out of the cistern. When he discovered that Joseph was missing, he tore his clothes in grief. Then he went back to his brothers and lamented, "The boy is gone! What will I do now?" (Genesis 37: 26–27, 29–30 NLT)

Joseph was gone, and Reuben's hopes of saving him were dashed. Not all Joseph's brothers apparently shared the same feelings of jealousy and contempt toward him. However, Joseph's story represents common themes that can apply to all families. Family dysfunction can happen in the lives of believers and non-believers. The same dynamics that contributed to the saga in Joseph's family still persist today. In the following pages, you'll find relational patterns and examples of familial dysfunction that open the door to unforgiveness.

FAMILY THEMES AND PATTERNS

Christmas. Thanksgiving. Birthdays. Reunions. Even a simple phone call or seeing a member of your family can sometimes trigger stress and anxiety. Just the mention of a family member's name can be enough to send you spiraling back down memory lane. It's no wonder that tension underlies so many family gatherings. Most families have not dealt with the quarrels, disagreements, and offenses that plague their household or lineage. And because our families shape our thoughts, reinforce our behaviors, and have a profound impact on our worldview, they can leave us with scars like no other and cause us to question whether the world is mean, the church is safe, and God is real.

Families should be a place of refuge and a safe space to share your heart. But many individuals ultimately end up seeking love and comfort from outsiders because their families have failed them. And there are so many types of family dysfunction that can lead to unforgiveness:

- **Abandonment**
- **Neglect**
- **Rejection**
- **Lack of communication**
- **Jealousy**
- **Favoritism**
- **Substance Abuse**
- **Patterns of Abuse** (physical, mental, sexual, verbal, emotional)

- Violence
- Divorce
- Mental Illness
- Manipulation
- Trauma

If we examine Joseph's family structure, his father, Jacob (also known as Israel), created an atmosphere that enabled jealousy, comparison, and neglect to grow. Joseph was the second youngest of twelve, and his father loved him more than his other sons. This favoritism was not Josephs' fault; his father chose to treat him differently. It was Jacob's responsibility as a parent to love all his children with the same intensity. This is just one example of how environments of strife and contention are born and flourish. If we examine Joseph's family tree further, we understand that Jacob's parents (Isaac and Rebekah) played favorites among their children as well. Rebekah favored Jacob while Isaac favored Esau. Using Jacob, Rebekah schemed to take the birthright or blessing from Esau, who was entitled to it as the elder brother, and give it to Jacob instead (see Genesis 16:17). When Esau learned that Jacob was given the blessing from his father in error, he vowed in anger to kill his brother Jacob.

See the pattern? From jealousy to deception and favoritism, family patterns (good or bad) can be passed down from generation to generation if they're not dealt with.

Seeds of discord can replicate and cause more harm if they are not dealt with instantly. Joseph's brothers allowed the cancer of jealousy to grow within them and become evil, deadly desires. Many individuals know that jealousy is a fruit that does not belong in the life of a believer, but they may allow it to linger anyway and put themselves in a dangerous position. Although the list is short, jealousy can have a profound effect individually and collectively:

- **Jealousy can cause you to make irrational decisions.**
- **Jealousy can add to the evil intentions that have taken root in your heart.**
- **Jealousy overshadows your unique calling and position.**
- **If left unchecked, jealousy can lead to death.**

While Joseph's brothers believed they had heard and seen the last of him, God had other plans. Plans already set in motion before they were born. They sold Joseph into slavery, but God used their wicked scheme to set him up for success.

"The Lord was with Joseph" (Genesis 39:2 NLT). Throughout his life, Joseph received assurances from God that He was always near. When his brothers betrayed him and he was falsely accused and imprisoned, God's commitment to him kept him going.

Your siblings or other family members may have mistreated you, or your parents may have harmed you, but when the Lord is with you, even time spent in jail can be used for good. God's definition of the success he's promised you does not exempt you from pain or wrongdoing. Nor does it imply that you will always "win." However, God's assurances give you an advantage when it comes to understanding how to get back up when life knocks you down. Having the Lord with him helped Joseph gain insight into his past and wisdom for the future. Joseph's imprisonment revealed several things about him, his family, and God:

- **Joseph gained wisdom about keeping things to himself, instead of bragging.**
- **Joseph understood that His life was not controlled by the hands of others.**
- **Joseph learned that God keeps His promises, no matter how long it takes.**
- **Joseph realized that forgiving his family was not by his strength, but the transformation completed in his heart by God.**

Joseph's prison experience prepared him for the miracle God performed in his heart, and the family breakthrough yet to come. Joseph was sold into slavery by his brothers at the age of seventeen. He endured betrayal by his brothers and Potiphar's wife (who falsely accused him) and was thrown into prison for a crime he didn't commit. Joseph helped a prison inmate, who forgot to mention Joseph at his time of release, which resulted in extra time spent in prison.

Thirteen years went by before Joseph saw his dreams and promise from God realized. Just as God had showed him, Joseph took his position as second-in-command of Egypt. While in his new role, wouldn't you know that the very family members who wronged him suddenly needed him because there was a famine and they were running out of food.

When the Hurt is Close

When Jacob learned that there was grain in Egypt, he said to his sons, "why do you just keep looking at each other?" He continued, "I have heard that there is grain in Egypt. Go down there and buy some for us, so that we may live and not die." . . . Now Joseph was the governor of the land, the one who sold grain to all its people. So when Joseph's brothers arrived, they bowed down to him with their faces to the ground. (Genesis 42:1–2, 6)

Joseph recognized them right away, but they had no clue he was the brother they had sold into slavery (see Genesis 42:7). God had certainly turned the tables, and His timing was impeccable! Just as He had shown Joseph in a dream, his family members bowed down to him. Years had gone by since he'd last seen his brothers, and I can imagine they were never far from his thoughts. The totality of his experience seems to come with such emotion as he recalled his road to the palace. The Word of God notes three moments where Joseph wept after revealing who he was to his siblings.

1. He turned away from them and began to **weep**, but then came back and spoke to them again. (Genesis 42:24)
2. Deeply moved at the sight of his brother, Joseph hurried out and looked for a place to **weep**. He went into his private room and **wept** there. (Genesis 43:30)
3. And he **wept** so loudly that the Egyptians heard him, and Pharaoh's household heard about it. (Genesis 45:2)

Perhaps seeing them triggered negative memories. Maybe, Joseph experienced painful flashbacks from all that had happened to him. Or perhaps he wept because he was so overwhelmed with praise and thanksgiving when he recalled his past. Or he may have wept with joy because he was so grateful to see his family again, despite their betrayal. Maybe it was all of the above.

Joseph was now in a different place mentally, spiritually, and emotionally. His maturity allowed him to reframe and view his experience through a spiritual lens.

For Jacob, reuniting with Joseph was a dream come true. The son whom he'd believed to be dead was actually alive! Not only was he alive, but Joseph reigned as second-in-command in Egypt. Once he'd laid eyes on his son, Jacob could die with peace. And with the death of their father, fear and worry overcame Joseph's brothers. Would Joseph mistreat them in the same manner that they'd mistreated him, now that their father was gone? By this time, his brothers knew their wrong and fully understood the consequences of their evil rejection. We can infer from the text that their long-ago scheme weighed them down. Much time had passed, but the memory of what they did never went away. For years, Joseph's brothers had witnessed the impact their evil toward Joseph had on their father. Jacob's heartbreak began with the absence of Joseph, and their family was never the same. Would Joseph seek revenge and vengeance for their betrayal?

> When Joseph's brothers saw that their father was dead, they said, "What if Joseph holds a grudge against us and pays us back for all the wrongs we did to him?" So they sent word to

Joseph, saying, "Your father left these instructions before he died: 'This is what you are to say to Joseph: I ask you to forgive your brothers the sins and the wrongs they committed in treating you so badly.' Now please forgive the sins of the servants of the God of your father." When their message came to him, Joseph wept. (Genesis 50:15–17)

They didn't realize that Joseph did not hold a grudge against them for their actions. Joseph found himself assuring his brothers that he had forgiven them. Joseph's famous saying in Genesis 50:20 gave solace and peace to their troubled hearts: "You intended to harm me, but God intended it for good to accomplish what is now being done, the saving of many lives" (NLT).

All that took place in Joseph's life appeared as though it were at the hands of his brothers. But it wasn't. God was in control of all that had happened to Joseph.

Your roots can grow deep in God when, just like Joseph, you realize that God, for better or worse, can use your family to accomplish His will in your life. Against all odds, God will place you where He's purposed you to be. And He will work a transformative miracle in those who have harmed you.

If God did it for Joseph, He can do it for you.

A WORD ON CHURCH HURT

The church was intended to represent an extension of our family. For many, the church is their first introduction *to* family, faith, and love. However, we live in a fallen world. And though many clergy wear the garment of leadership and may even love Christ, they do not override God's judgment or His discipline. Nor are they blameless and above the law.

Many individuals find it very difficult to forgive those within the church who behave hypocritically. When pain comes explicitly from those who are religious, many feel torn, betrayed, and deeply wounded. Make no mistake about it; church hurt is undeniable. Wounds from those who believe in Jesus can shape how you view other believers, pastors, love, and the church as a whole. Unresolved church hurt may tempt you to consider the lie that the church isn't credible or is completely against you. Why do people become greatly offended when the perpetrator or enemy hails from the body of Christ? **I believe that offense within the church can most often be attributed to expectations.**

That's not to say people within the body of Christ shouldn't be subject to healthy expectations. But Scripture highlights that there are differences between those who are babes in Christ versus individuals who are mature in Christ (see Hebrews 5:12–14). God's Word also provides clear guidance on how to identify masqueraders and false prophets who don't practice what they preach.

While many individuals understand that no one is perfect, some get amnesia or turn a blind eye to the reality that members within the church are spiritually sick. They too need healing. Christianity is not a race. It is a process, birthed by faith and taught, refined, and graced by imperfect people. Christians are called to develop through discipleship, evidenced by personal intentionality and sound biblical doctrine from the church. Unfortunately, some have chosen to place their hearts in the wrong hands, believing they are secure.

Dear friends, please remember: An individual may have been called by God to speak into your life, befriend you, or become your pastor. But they were never called to be your savior.

"*They* should know better." I've not only heard those words but have said them myself. This utterance has become all too common, as people have chosen to separate from the church because of hurt feelings, betrayals, and offense. Many find themselves unwilling to forgive because they were harmed by power-drunk clergy leaders or manipulative and opportunistic church members—individuals who chose to prey on new converts, the young, the vulnerable, and the weak. People who use words of flattery, yet they are full of discord.

Like you, I've certainly been there.

Yes, I've been harmed by the church. But I've also experienced healing within the church.

As the body of Christ, we're called to stand out and be different than the rest of the world. We gather together to celebrate our shared love of Christ and unity among fellow believers. But please realize, no matter how good they appear, behave, or sound, discernment will always be necessary to root out those who are insincere or have ulterior motives. While no excuses or bargaining should happen when individuals intentionally harm others, those touched by church hurt must remember that Christians are spiritually flawed on different levels.

No matter what happens, God has made His Word available to all. Anyone can study, apply, and be discipled by it. Therefore, He holds every individual accountable to His Word, not to the works of other people.

Whenever you make decisions from your place of pain, you're more apt to react in error than in reason.

Christians are not immune from sin or harm from within the church. However, focusing on becoming more mature in Christ is no excuse to avoid practicing discernment within the church. When we place our ultimate expectation in Christ, we can approach church members with a different outlook. Like you, they are trying to become more like Christ, which is a continual process of refinement and sanctification.

The advantage of being a Christ follower is knowing that God doesn't place a period on your pain, no matter the source of your harm.

FURTHER ENCOURAGEMENT

Dear friend, I don't know why you experienced hurt and harm from your family or church members. I can't imagine what you've gone through or how it's affected all the areas of your life. I don't know why, and I don't know how, but I can tell you that what you've gone through is being used to further the story of your life. Through all the suffering you've endured, a stronger character is being birthed. God is not surprised at what happened, nor does it represent who He is. But just as He was for Joseph, God is with you. He was with you when it happened, and He saw what happened to you. And though it may have physically and emotionally harmed you, it did not damage your soul. Let God be your anchor, and allow Him to heal everywhere you're hurting.

Forgive the ones who are responsible for forcing you to navigate the rough waters of life. Forgive those who should have been your biggest cheerleaders but weren't. Forgive those who could have been your best friends but excluded you. Forgive the ones whose job it was to love and instruct you in the right way but failed. Forgive those who attempted to do the best they could with their knowledge and resources. Forgive those who are blinded and deceived by jealousy. Forgive those who didn't speak up on your behalf. Forgive those who saw your suffering and yet chose to remain silent. Forgive those who intentionally harmed you. Forgive those who abandoned you. Forgive those who wanted to but did not know how. Forgive those who knew how yet did not want to.

Forgive them.

As they did for Joseph, may these words ring true in your heart as you release offense and place your family member(s) and members of the church in the hands of God:

> "Don't be afraid of me. Am I God, that I can punish you? You intended to harm me, but God intended it all for good. He brought me to this position so I could save the lives of many people." (Genesis 50:19–20 NLT).

The Forgiving Tip #6

When you give God your past, He redeems the time you thought you'd lost.

Reflection Scripture

Instead of shame and dishonor, you will enjoy a double share of honor. You will possess a double portion of prosperity in your land, and everlasting joy will be yours.
Isaiah 61:7 NLT

❧ Take A Moment ❧

Reflect

1) The patterns I see in my family are:
2) I can set healthier boundaries by:

Act

- Ask God to show you how to set healthier boundaries for yourself within your family and began to implement them.
- Ask God for wisdom and discernment in choosing the right church and believers you can trust.

Prayer

Dear Lord,

Thank You for forming me in my mother's womb. Thank You for healing me of the wounds caused by family and other believers. I may not understand why You chose to place me with a family who would cause me so much pain and strife, but I know that You are a God who sits high and looks low. I believe the wrongs done will be made right—in Your timing and Your way. I put my hope and faith in You. Thank You for showing me that I belong to a family of believers who are not perfect but strive to live for You. Thank You for revealing that although this family may forsake me, You will embrace me. You've called me by name, and I am Your own. I am Your son or daughter whom You love with an everlasting love. Thank You for illuminating those dark places that have caused much grief. Thank You for Your healing balm. Thank you for taking my offense and pain and transforming the dysfunction into purpose. Thank You for using me to be the bondage breaker in my family so that You may be glorified. There's no wrong in my life that You cannot heal. Thank You for prayers answered, reconciliation, and the wholeness that You're bringing into my life, my family, and the church. You are a miracle worker!

In Jesus's name,

Amen

chapter 7

When it Doesn't Make Sense

> *Don't let any experience drive a wedge between you and God.*
> ~New Living Translation Commentary, 2nd Ed.

EVEN THE BEST work of Hollywood fiction could never compare to Job's story in the Bible. The lessons and insights it offers remain transformative and timeless.

The book of Job chronicles one man's life that was turned completely upside down. Job was hand-picked by God to endure monumental suffering because he was "doing it right," which led him to question God, wallow in depression, and wish he was never born. He struggled with comprehending "why" and never received an answer.

In short, Job's story is our story.

We know that God is good. He's *more* than good. God has the resume and history to justify His sovereignty, faithfulness, and goodness. But when you read the book of Job and see what God allowed to happen to him, you may think He's anything but good. In one moment, everything was taken from Job. First his possessions and family were stripped from him in a matter of minutes. And just when he thought it was over, there was even more drama.

Job was the richest man in the land. A man of integrity and prayer who hated sin and loved holiness. A righteous man who took care of his family, even praying for his children on their behalf when they sinned against God. The Bible says he prayed regularly for his family. He believed and trusted in God. However, his trust in God became the basis for a test he didn't sign up for.

At the beginning of Job's story, we find the enemy roaming around the earth, completely oblivious to who Job is. That is, until God bragged about him.

> "Where have you come from?" the LORD asked Satan. Satan answered the LORD, "I have been patrolling the earth, watching everything that's going on." Then the LORD asked Satan, "Have you noticed my servant Job? He is the finest man in all the earth. He is blameless—a man of complete integrity. He fears God and stays away from evil." (Job 1:7–8 NLT)

You heard right. God raved about Job to the enemy. His track record caused God to give him a positive review. In response, Satan made the false accusation that Job's obedience and devotion to God were all due to a hedge of protection around him, his family, and his wealth. Satan went on to claim, that without God's security and favor, Job's allegiance to God would diminish.

> "You have always put a wall of protection around him and his home and his property. You have made him prosper in everything he does. Look how rich he is! But reach out and take away everything he has, and he will surely curse you to your face!" "All right you may test him," the LORD said to Satan. "Do whatever you want with everything he possesses, but don't harm him physically." (Job 1:10–12 NLT)

Satan challenged God, not Job. In turn, God trusted Job to disprove the enemy's accusation that Job's loyalty depended on what he could get from Him. Poor Job. He had no idea what the enemy had in store. Also, he was clueless that God chose him to prove the enemy wrong. Satan assumed Job's commitment was fake, but God knew that Job would respond favorably and pass the test.

Test #1: In one day, the Bible makes a note of Job's farmhands killed by the Sabeans, 500 teams of oxen, 500 donkeys, and 3,000 camels stolen. Also, 7,000 sheep were killed along with their shepherds in a fire. Lastly, his sons and daughters died when their brother's house collapsed during a feast they were attending there (see Job 1:13–19).

In *one day,* immense tragedy struck. The enemy killed his family and stole his wealth. One after another, four messengers delivered news that turned his world upside down. Hearing that news would be enough to make anyone ask why and get angry at God. But Job didn't. His words proved Satan's accusations to be false:

> "I came naked from my mother's womb, and I will be naked when I leave. The LORD gave me what I had and the LORD has taken it away. Praise the name of the LORD!" In all of this, Job did not sin by blaming God. (Job 1:21–22 NLT)

With a grieving heart, Job passed the first test. He did so without blaming God, and he showed the enemy that his devotion to God did not hinge on what he received *from* God.

Test #2: Like clockwork, Satan was roaming around the earth like before; and again, God presented him with an offer he could not refuse: "Have you noticed my servant Job?" (see Job 2:1–3). Once more, Satan made his case for why he could not get to Job:

> "Skin for skin!" Satan answered the LORD. A man will give up everything he owns in exchange for his life. But stretch out and take away his health, and he will surely curse You to your face." "Very well," the LORD told Satan, "he is in your

power; only spare his life." So Satan left the LORD's presence and struck Job with terrible boils from head to foot. (Job 2:4–7 NLT)

Why would God offer Job to Satan again? Because God had confidence in Job. Job displayed a servant's heart. It was apparent that his affection and reverence for God took prominence in his life. After God gave Satan the green light, Job became afflicted; not only physically but emotionally and mentally as well, to the point that he was nearly overwhelmed. Job's response was undoubtedly different than his first test. Although he didn't blame God, Job cursed the day he was born (see Job 3:1).

Job became an emotionally torn outcast because of everything that had taken place. His wife suggested he curse God and die, and his friends, who were initially silent, began to rationalize that his sufferings were brought on by sin. And still, God remained silent. From our perspective, Job was in a bad place. From God's vantage point, he was right where God wanted him to be. In spite of all he'd lost and the deterioration of his physical health, Job was still alive.

Job remained oblivious to the reason for his trials, completely unaware that God was counting on him to prove the enemy wrong. Job, a man who did no wrong, became both a pawn and the starring figure in this dramatic saga.

This story mirrors our relationship with God and the way we question why things happen. It leaves us examining the depths of our faith when, on the surface, it appears that God has failed us. Through Job's emotional journey, we get a sense of the potential magnitude of unanswered questions. It reveals our hidden grudges against God and what we believe about Him. God's silence gives us insight into how resentment can turn into anger toward Him. We also gain insight into how we can become distant from the only One who can help. And most of all, we discover that God is still good, even when our circumstances are not.

The book of Job contains three significant lessons we can take solace in and find encouragement to drop our offenses with God:

1. God is in control.
2. Satan has limits.
3. Satan cannot do what God forbids him from doing.

Those are reasons to rejoice! Even though your heart aches from your circumstances, understanding the sovereignty of God should provide some relief. By sparing Job's life, God placed limits on what could happen while he was being tested. Satan could take anything from Job and physically harm him, but he could not take Job's life. God allowed it. He *allowed* Job's devastation. If anyone had cause to demand an explanation from God, it was Job.

This upright man who obeyed God and loved and took care of his home, became the central figure in Satan's attempts to silence him and discredit God.

When we don't understand why something happens, we become vulnerable to doubting God and taking offense with Him. Will you continue to walk steadfastly with God, even when His sovereignty hurts?

That was Job's real test, and that continues to be the test in your life.

During times of testing, our hearts become most vulnerable as we attempt to wrestle with our realities and hold on to what we know about God. Our valley experiences reveal our grit, or they expose our deficiencies. When we want to persevere and pass the test, the overwhelming desire to "figure it out" may keep us from moving forward.

That is, if you get stuck at the "why." But God, *why* did it happen? God, *why* did You let that happen? How could You? When God allows circumstances, people, or things to harm us, our natural and human response is to ask Him that one-word question that many often fear. Even in Christian circles, you may hear repeatedly, "Never ask God why"—as if God doesn't know. We may not say it with our lips, but our heart longs to receive an answer that could rationalize our problems. Or . . . Just. Make. Sense. Could God be testing our faith, even when our "why" isn't answered?

MY TEST OF FAITH

"How can I trust Him again when He allowed it?" Tears fell down my face as I tried to pray and make sense of what *didn't* happen. A year prior, I took on the challenge of adopting the Daniel Fast (a three-week commitment to eating mostly fruits and vegetables for spiritual enrichment, based on Daniel's fasting habits in the Bible) at the beginning of the year. I wanted more of Him, to understand what the year 2017 would bring, and desired answers to my prayers. I wasn't a novice at fasting, but my desire to "take it up a notch" spiritually and hear Him without distraction was my motivation. For twenty-one days, I became more purposeful in seeking Him.

I went without foods that I enjoyed, drank only water, and ate plant-based meals. I expanded my prayer life, and my time spent reading Scripture and being in God's presence increased—all for the sole purpose of knowing Him more intimately. Day twenty-one arrived, and while joyously reflecting on all that had occurred during my fast, I said, "God, if You don't answer *that* prayer, it's fine. I feel so complete in You and have grown closer to You than ever before."

Right after I made that statement, as if on cue, the phone rang. That phone conversation led me to believe something new was beginning to manifest. Filled with excitement, I presumed that God was finally providing an answer to my longings.

I had grown accustomed to having prayers answered right after a fast, so it was easy to assume that the phone call was God's latest answer. From that conversation, a new hope was born. Eager and amazed at His timely response, I was thankful and in awe of the new door that I thought He had opened.

I thought wrong.

When it Doesn't Make Sense

Six months after the Daniel Fast, I replayed that phone conversation over and over again and thought about all the empty promises I'd believed. I tried to understand. I wanted to comprehend, to make sense of what happened and why. With a wounded heart, questions unanswered, and hope deferred, I found it difficult to fast and pray again. I just could not. In June of that year, the Holy Spirit answered me at 2:00 a.m. while I was lying in bed.

"What do you think about tests, Dionnea?"

I couldn't deny *not* hearing those words as they spoke to my heart. *Test? God, that was a TEST? But why? Why did you allow it? Do you know how much that meant to me? How could you?*

Now that I had *some* explanation, I certainly wasn't pleased with what He'd said. To say that I was angry with God would have been an understatement. I was heartbroken and couldn't believe it. When I'd fasted before, He had always provided an answer the next day. I was counting on Him to answer me in the same way he had before, and I never fathomed that He would allow me to be tested *after* I'd willingly sought Him. I was trying to do the right thing, and *this* is what happened? I now realize just how much we place God in a box based on our past encounters with Him. We assume that we know what He'll do, how He's going to respond, and when.

I couldn't understand how God could allow me to be tested during my first Daniel Fast. His revelation that one of my prayer request answers was a test left me speechless. Hurt, sadness, and disappointment clouded my mind and heart as I wrestled with the question of why. In the days and months that followed, my prayers were half-hearted, and attempts at fasting again proved to be complicated.

Fear, instead of faith, became my central focus. I didn't want to consider the possibility of fasting again, only to have my hopes dashed.

I just couldn't bring myself to do it.

How could I trust Him? I desperately wanted to, but I grieved the outcome and what He would allow in the future. A part of me felt deceived by God. If He could do *this*, then who can I trust?

With the start of another new year, 2018 brought me a sense of renewed hope. Hurt and sadness slowly subsided as I felt more courageous to attempt fasting again. My desire to hear God clearly and submit to His sovereignty motivated my pursuit. However, to my surprise, these attempts failed as well, and I noticed my heart wasn't fully committed. At last, I became brave enough to ask God about reasons why my efforts to fast seemed so futile. And once again, He answered in the quietness of the night—right before I drifted off to sleep.

"Dionnea, you're stuck at the WHY."

God used the very words I'd already written for this chapter to open my eyes to my dilemma. Yes, I was stuck and couldn't see my way forward without knowing why. Why had He tested me? Why had He *wanted* to test me? If He wasn't the author of this test, why did He allow it? Waiting on God's promise for over ten years wasn't enough? Feeling as though He'd challenged me with a test already in progress that caused me such pain made it difficult to comprehend His goodness.

Have you ever felt this way? He may not have been the author of my test, but He didn't stop it either.

Would I believe God to be the Promise Keeper still, or would I assume He had failed me and proven Himself to be a liar? When we stand at the crossroads of our faith and endure the silence, the waiting, or His answer of no, our attitude in the end reflects the condition of our hearts better than in times of abundance and certainty.

What I now understand about that experience lies more in the process of the testing than having my longing fulfilled.

So many find themselves struggling with this same challenge.

Many people find themselves stuck at the WHY.

Why was that prayer not answered or that loved one not healed?

Why were they blessed, but I'm still sitting in the waiting room?

Why her/him, and not me?

Why, **God,** *why?*

The enemy loves that you're stuck. He loves that you're stuck questioning why as you continue to build a silent resentment toward God. He wants you to remain anchored in your anger toward Him.

We get stuck in trying to figure it out.

We get stuck in hopelessness.

We get stuck by blaming God instead of the enemy.

We get stuck by comparing our lives to others'.

When you're stuck at the "why," you cannot move forward into the life God has designed for you.

Trying to rationalize and make sense of our circumstances leaves us with sleepless nights, debilitating headaches, and a racing mind that won't let go. Our hearts break when the One who could stop our testing chooses not to—and when His answer doesn't come right away or at all. It's confusing, hurtful, and, let's be real—it's just not fair. When bad things happen to good people, their hope grows weary from the battle scars they receive. It becomes easy for the mind to grow idle, and many lose faith *because* of unanswered questions.

But the truth is, God can allow testing without warning and without asking. He can do that because He's God. It does not matter if you've walked with Him for years or are involved in ministry. No one is exempt. However, dear friends, please remember that God never allows a test that's without purpose. Regardless if you understand it now, later, or in eternity.

When experiences do not line up with our expectations of God, we can choose to abandon Him because of unanswered questions. We can lose hope, and depression can quickly become a friend when we can't dissect or analyze the reason why things happen. One important thing I have discovered, especially in times of uncertainty, is this: **The why can be powerful, but the Who has power over ALL.**

When it Doesn't Make Sense

The book of Job is a sobering reminder that no matter what obstacle God allows in your life, He is bigger than your question of "why." The only way to get unstuck is by putting God back in His proper position: at the center of your life—above the emotions, misunderstandings, and attempts to figure it out.

When you realize that some questions will go unanswered, you reconcile your "why."
By releasing your "why," you can become more acquainted with the Who—which is God. Then the peace of God can flow into your life. It's humbling, revelatory, and displays our trust in Him.

When relief from suffering appears to be nowhere in sight, will you find fault with God? Some people can go days, months, or years with a heart hardened against God. I believe many find themselves in this position and suffer silently. Job's life reveals how we approach trials and grief. It reveals our perspectives about God and erases the misconceptions we have concerning our Christianity. It can leave us feeling as though our faith is at ground zero.

Like Job, we will inevitably stand at the crossroads of our faith. We can either be angry and stay angry at God for what He allowed, or we can let our "whys" and God's silence drive our faith.

Will you give up on God, or will you press into God?

Will you allow what happened to override your faith in God's goodness?

Will you allow what didn't happen to stop you from trusting God?

If you give up on God, you'll still have your problem and question why. But if you stand with Him in faith, your issues can become the building blocks to the path that leads to your breakthrough. The only One who knew Job would come out of these trials with more than he started was God.

Like Job, we're called to deepen our faith. The solution to relieving your unanswered questions lies in choosing Him over your need to know. It requires a deepening of your faith in Christ.

Faith doesn't require understanding. If we understood, our need for faith would not exist. Instead, faith calls us to lean in and stand on God's promises. It beckons us to find out more of who God is, no matter our present circumstances. This sifting process can come at any time and in any way. Many have forfeited their hand and folded out of hopelessness. The test pushed them too far and shook their foundation of faith. If that is the current position you find yourself in, you're in a great place to pick up the pieces and start rebuilding your trust. If you're tempted to give up, please don't.

Don't fold.

Reject offense.

Reject depression.

Reject the lies from the enemy.

Reject suffering as being the final answer.

Reject the lie that God doesn't know what's going on.

Reject the lie that He's not concerned or doesn't care.

Reject the lie that His silence is deceptive.
Don't resent God.

God doesn't *need* your forgiveness. But "forgive God" for allowing your test to come. How do you do this? By releasing your questions of "why" in faith, and trusting Him for the outcome. God has an excellent track record—unblemished and undefeated.
You can trust Him.

You may not be able to see it now or fully believe it, but thank God that He considered you worthy to take the test. God knew what the devil did not know—that Job would pass the test. And God has said the same about you. But he knows the way that I take; when he has tested me, I will come forth as gold. (Job 23:10)

In the end, Job received more than he started with. No, he couldn't get his children back. Nevertheless, God blessed him with even more children and finances than before. Job was now the richest man in the land (see Job 42:10-16).

Out of all things Job received in the end, his suffering produced a deeper level of intimacy with God and birthed a deeper level of worship within him. Job knew God at the beginning of his story, but he didn't *know* God. Job's questions never received an answer, but God revealed a facet of His Sovereignty that Job had never experienced.

This test was designed to show you and the enemy what you're made of. God tailored it to uncover areas of strength and weakness. When it doesn't make sense, be even more determined to make it to the other side. Express to God how much it hurts and how you may feel betrayed that He allowed it to happen. But in your venting, keep in mind God's impeccable character.

No matter what you're going through, don't let it steal your faith in Him and mis-shape your view of Him.

He is God and does not change. He is good and kind. He's always been good, even during your darkest days.

The Forgiving Tip #7

When you let go of the why, you become more acquainted with the Who—God.

Reflection Scripture

Then Job replied to the LORD: "I know that you can do anything, and no one can stop you. You asked, 'Who is this that questions my wisdom with such ignorance?' It is I—and I was talking about things I knew nothing about, things far too wonderful for me. You said, 'Listen and I will speak! I have some questions for you, and you must answer them.' I had only heard about you before, but now I have seen you with my own eyes."

Job 42:1–5 NLT

❧ Take A Moment ❧

Reflect

1) I believe that God is:

2) I can strengthen my relationship with God by:

Act

- Research the names of God and scriptures related to His character. Often an electronic search of His name or aspect of His character will be accompanied by scriptures.
- Make a list and compare His names to how He's shown up in your life.

Prayer

Dear Lord,

Thank You for keeping me. Thank You for being patient with me and drawing me closer to You. I admit this experience of suffering has been hard to navigate. I'm hurting, upset, and struggle with making sense of it. I acknowledge that I don't understand the heaviness that has lingered in me for far too long. Lord, I know that I shouldn't feel offended by You, but I am, and I'm weary. However, I will cling to You and trust You despite what I feel and think. I recognize that You're not doing this to me. But, in ways that I don't see, You're doing it for me. I may not receive an answer soon, or on this side of eternity. Nevertheless, I choose to drop my offense toward You and press in to know You more. Lord, You've been good, kind, and merciful to me. You said in Jeremiah 33:3, "Call to me, and

I will answer you and tell you great and unsearchable things you do not know." You also said in James 1:5, "If any of you lacks wisdom, you should ask God." Lord, I feel as though I'm walking through the valley of the shadow of death, but I know You are with me. I look to You, because I know even in silence You're with me. I may never understand why, but may I always cling to Who—You, Lord. The Author and Finisher of my faith.

In Jesus's name,

Amen

chapter 8

When Grace and Mercy Follow Me

> *There is therefore now no condemnation to them which* are in Christ Jesus, *who do not walk according to the flesh, but according to the Spirit.*
>
> ~Romans 8:1 NKJV

REGRET, GUILT, SHAME, and sorrow. If King David could have turned back the hands of time, knowing what the outcome would be, would he have made different choices? If *we* knew the repercussions of our choice(s) before making a decision, would we think twice about the path we choose? Sometimes, the worst offender is us. *How did I get here . . . again?* we ask ourselves. Sometimes, it's not what others have done to you but what you've done to yourself. And yes, there are times we fall into temptation, believing that our choices will produce the desires we want. We walk into situations, thinking we know all the facts, and proceed with naïve hope—only to end up in tears.

We all can name moments when regret has caused us heavy hearts. When you're the offender, blame can become burdensome, and you may continue through life asking "What if?" We drag our sin and shame around, constantly condemning our shortcomings. We live in regret and fail to realize that the weight of yesterday keeps us from flying high. We are offended by our actions and cannot see a way around them, and we become our own worst enemy as we wrestle with living out God's best plan for our lives. Yes, now and then the biggest offender in our lives is difficult to ignore—because it's us.

For David, one decision sparked a series of tragic events, and he had no one to blame but himself. Handpicked by God at the age of thirteen, David was set apart for an important task: He was chosen to reign and become Israel's next king. God didn't choose him because of his perfection. He chose him because his heart of submission and dedication to God was visible. God planned to use David to lead Israel and set an example for others.

Because of his spiritual posture with God, the anointing on David's life was evident even at a young age. David began with the right motives. Following God's leading as a young boy and well into adulthood, David learned from King Saul. The leadership roles and responsibilities the king gave him prepared him for his future task. While he didn't take the throne until the age of thirty, David still learned skills for battle, how to follow by submitting, and insight into what it takes to be an effective leader. He knew God, loved Him, and desired to serve Him.

But as set apart as he was, David was still a man.

Like David, we're prone to mistakes and temptation. Likely to react impulsively instead of thinking things through. We're subject to being motivated by our feelings instead of wisdom. We choose to momentarily forget all that we've been taught and second-guess doing the right thing. All it takes is one moment—one poor choice—for your life and the lives of those around you to change in disastrous ways.

One day, David made such a choice. A critical decision that began with disobedience in his heart. Indeed, it led to more than he bargained for and cost him significantly. If he had only known the impact of his choice, David surely would have chosen otherwise.

DAVID'S STORY

Instead of going out to battle like other kings, David stayed home.

> Then it happened in the spring, at the time when kings go out to battle, that David sent Joab and his servants with him and all Israel, and they destroyed the sons of Ammon and besieged Rabbah. But David stayed at Jerusalem. (2 Samuel 11:1 NASB)

On that day, David chose to forego his responsibility to lead in favor of leisure. It's possible that exhaustion got the best of him or he believed his absence on the battlefield would be less noticeable. Maybe he thought his troops could handle it. After all, they were not novices when it came to getting the job done, and they were well prepared. Years spent as a king and doing the work of God may have caused him to adopt an attitude of entitlement. Perhaps he thought he deserved to have a day off. Whatever his reasoning, he fell into the trap of temptation that proved to be detrimental. Disobedience deterred him, and pride deceived him into believing he could have it all—at any moment and any cost. David was king. He could do what he wanted and when. He had no one to answer to . . . except for God.

In the days that followed his decision to stay in Jerusalem, his example of leadership became a lesson of what *not* to do. **David's story demonstrates that even those who are hand-picked by God are not without sin. And sometimes, their fall is so impactful that it reaches those who are not directly connected to them.**

Rising from his nap in the evening, David stood at his balcony and looked across the land. His gaze fell on Bathsheba as she was bathing. Instantly, he was mesmerized. Her beauty was so hypnotic. Temptation knocked on the door, and David answered when he should have fled. At that moment, all logical thinking for him ceased.

After inquiring, David knew she was a married woman. But he still wanted her. He *had* to have her, no matter the cost.

He saw.

He lusted.

He got what he wanted.

Now when evening came David arose from his bed and walked around on the roof of the king's house, and from the roof he saw a woman bathing; and the woman was very beautiful in appearance. So David sent and inquired about the woman. And one said, "Is this not Bathsheba, the daughter of Eliam, the wife of Uriah the Hittite?" David sent messengers and took her, and when she came to him, he lay with her; and when she had purified herself from her uncleanness, she returned to her house. The woman conceived; and she sent and told David, and said, "I am pregnant." (2 Samuel 11:2–5 NASB)

Why didn't Bathsheba say no? When we consider the time period, the role of domestic woman, and Bathsheba's role as a subject of the king, she would have faced grave consequences if she'd said no—including death. She had to obey the king of the land. Adding insult to injury, Bathsheba's husband Uriah was a soldier in David's army. She and Uriah were both obligated to do whatever the king said, even if they didn't want to.

Individuals that God entrusts in leadership positions are extremely vulnerable to temptation and pride. They can be tempted to do things when no one is watching and can develop an ego that seduces them into believing they could have it all and answer to no one. David's impulsive actions may have surprised him, but God, who searches all hearts, saw it coming (see Jeremiah 17:10). He knew David would not resist the invitation to commit adultery.

To cover up his affair and the resulting pregnancy, David ordered the commanding officer, Joab, to kill Uriah.

> In the morning David wrote a letter to Joab and sent it by the hand of Uriah. He had written in the letter, saying, "Place Uriah in the front line of the fiercest battle and withdraw from him, so that he may be struck down and die." (2 Samuel 11:14–15 NASB)

God wasn't surprised at what David did.
God was not surprised at what you did either.

CORRECTION AND CONSEQUENCES

God can see around the corner before we get there, and He sees our sins long before we commit them. Because God is all knowing, He knew *before* He called David to the throne that he would fall into temptation, lie, and murder an innocent man. Yet, God still called him a man after God's own heart (see Acts 13:22). How could this be? How did David qualify to be called by God in this manner? David's qualifications do not include perfection, but he compensated with a great desire to remain submitted and keep his heart pliable in God's hands—even when his flesh got in the way.

David's heart was turned to God.
David had faith in God.

David was committed to God.

David had a strong relationship with God.

David was anointed and appointed by God for these reasons. Being the youngest of his brothers, God considered him worthy and set apart—all because of his heart. Although David wasn't perfect, God knew his heart was pure and teachable.

But after his sin, David carried on with life as though nothing happened. Bathsheba mourned the death of Uriah, and the Bible states that after the end of her mourning period, David married her. David had entangled himself in deceit, attempting to cover his wrongdoing with lies and false perceptions. However, nothing gets past God. He used the prophet, Nathan, to get David's attention regarding his sins.

So the LORD sent Nathan the prophet to tell David this story. "There were two men in a certain town. One was rich, and one was poor. The rich man owned a great many sheep and cattle. The poor man owned nothing but one little lamb he had bought. He raised the little lamb, and it grew up with his children. It ate from the man's own plate and drank from his cup. He cuddled it in his arms like a baby daughter. One day a guest arrived at the home of the rich man. But instead of killing an animal from his own flock or herd, he took the poor man's lamb and killed it and prepared it for his guest."

David was furious. "As surely as the LORD lives," he vowed, "any man who would do such a thing deserves to die!

He must repay four lambs to the poor man for the one he stole and for having no pity."

Then Nathan said to David, "You are that man! The LORD, the God of Israel, says: I anointed you king of Israel and saved you from the power of Saul. I gave you your master's house and his wives and the kingdoms of Israel and Judah. And if that had not been enough, I would have given you much, much more. Why, then, have you despised the word of the LORD and done this horrible deed? For you have murdered Uriah the Hittite with the sword of the Ammonites and stolen his wife. From this time on, your family will live by the sword because you have despised me by taking Uriah's wife to be your own.

"This is what the LORD says: Because of what you have done, I will cause your own household to rebel against you. I will give your wives to another man before your very eyes, and he will go to bed with them in public view. You did it secretly, but I will make this happen to you openly in the sight of all Israel." (2 Samuel 12:1–12 NLT)

God is serious about sin. David assumed he could get away with it, but God sees all. Some consequences cannot be undone. They can leave permanent reminders of the choices you've made. It happened to David and may be happening with you.

Then David confessed to Nathan, "I have sinned against the LORD." Nathan replied, "Yes but the LORD has forgiven you, and you won't die for this sin. Nevertheless, because you have shown utter contempt for the LORD by doing this, your child will die." (2 Samuel 12:13–14 NLT)

A woman or man of character admits their failures as well as their successes. David's story demonstrates both how to and how *not* to lead by example. It also shows us that we can rise again from our downfalls. His story is an endless reminder that our little choices may not be so little at all. Their impact can be massive. **One bad seed can yield a harvest of consequences.**

It was settled. Because of David's sin, God's punishment was that his son would die. Forgiveness from God is available to us when we repent. However, there is no stopping the natural and spiritual consequences God has decreed. Yes, it's crucial to know that God doesn't play around when it comes to sin.

Nevertheless, God's judgment does not overshadow or remove His love. To accept and love God is to fully understand that God is loving, as well as just. If we only focus on His love or judgment alone, we fail to get to know Him intimately. A balance of love and discipline is the basis of all healthy parent-child relationships.

The truth is, we can make promises to avoid wrongdoing. But can we truly predict our response when we're faced with opportunities and pressure to sin? Some will turn away from sin, but others will fall into circumstances they'd always vowed to resist.

The choices we make may be related to our level of thinking, education, hope, and momentary desires. Regardless, there's no changing the past. The question becomes, what will do you do with the rest of the time you have left? Will you spend it in shame and regret? Or will you spend it wisely by applying what you're learning, as life continues to unfold?

Regrets can leave you stuck with thoughts of "if only."

Guilt can leave you with never-ending shame.

Sin can leave you separated from God.

When we fail in our obedience to God, and when our sin takes us away from being in His good standing, we create rifts in our relationship with Him. Our sins and the holiness of God cannot coexist. David's sin had grave consequences, but like a great leader, David demonstrates how we can restore our relationship to God through repentance.

Maybe you're left with consequences so dire, they follow you daily. Maybe you're beating yourself up as guilt, shame, and regret continue to hold you hostage. Perhaps others are reminding you of what you've done and how it's affecting them. Friend, I'm here to tell you that it ends today. The enemy would love to continue using your past sins to keep you in bondage and withhold forgiveness from yourself. Don't give him what he wants.

David couldn't change the past, but he fought for his future. How did he do it?

- David took ownership of what he did.

- David confessed his sins and repented to God.
- David accepted God's forgiveness and rejoiced.

Psalm 51 is a beautiful echo of David's sorrow over the wrong he committed. In this prayer, David laid his sin and heart out for God. He held nothing back, as he knew the only One who could help was ultimately the One he had wronged.

Have mercy on me, O God, because of your unfailing love. Because of your great compassion, blot out the stain of my sins. Wash me clean from my guilt. Purify me from my sin. For I recognize my rebellion; it haunts me day and night. Against you, and you alone, have I sinned; I have done what is evil in your sight. You will be proved right in what you say, and your judgement against me is just. For I was born a sinner—yes, from the moment my mother conceived me. But you desire honesty from the womb, teaching me wisdom even there.
Purify me from my sins, and I will be clean; wash me, and I will be whiter than snow. Oh, give me back my joy again; you have broken me—now let me rejoice. Don't keep looking at my sins. Remove the stain of my guilt. Create in me a clean hart, O God. Renew a loyal spirit within me. Do not banish me from your presence, and don't take your Holy Spirit from me. Restore to me the joy of your salvation, and make me willing to obey you. Then I will teach your ways to rebels, and they will return to you. Forgive me for shedding

blood, O God who saves; then I will joyfully sing of your forgiveness. Unseal my lips, O Lord, that my mouth may praise you. You do not desire a sacrifice, or I would offer one. You do not want a burnt offering. The sacrifice you desire is a broken spirit. You will not reject a broken and repentant heart, O God. (Psalm 51:1–17 NLT)

David's sin tore a family apart, killed an innocent man, broke his relationship with God, and birthed a child who later died. David's admission of guilt gave evidence of his choices that grieved him. However, David also showed us how to respond to God when we fall and what to do after we get up again.

There is no sin so great that God cannot forgive or heal.

This prayer of vulnerability and confession highlights why David was chosen and labeled by God as "a man after his own heart." Yes, he made mistakes, but David's heart was sold out to God, and he was genuinely sorry for what he'd done. Because God's grace and mercy took center stage in his life, David's other psalms reveal how to rejoice when God forgives and restores fellowship with us.

David was shown mercy when God did not give him what he deserved.

David was showered with grace when he realized that he could not save himself.

In God's loving kindness, He extends the same grace and mercy to us when we confess and repent wholeheartedly and call on His name.

If David had stayed unrepentant toward God, wallowed in self-pity, and chosen not to forgive himself and refused God's forgiveness, he still would have sinned against God. Why? **By placing your sin above God, you believe that it has more power *than* God. Essentially, you are demonstrating that you believe *His* forgiveness is not enough to cover what you've done.**

After praying to God for forgiveness, some never *feel* forgiven. The enemy would love to keep you trapped in believing that God does not forgive you. However, as Christ followers, you can't allow your feelings to have the final authority. Instead, you must let God's truth be your driving force and motivator. Embrace *this* truth and let it resonate within your heart: "There is therefore now no condemnation to them which are in Christ Jesus, who do not walk according to the flesh, but according to the Spirit" (Romans 8:1 NKJV).

Release the burden of guilt, shame, and condemnation. Experience the joy of God's forgiveness.

Forgive yourself for making that wrong decision.

Forgive yourself for causing harm (intentional or not) to others.

Forgive yourself for being disobedient to God.

Forgive yourself for choosing to do wrong.

Forgive yourself for seeing all the signs but ignoring them.

Forgive yourself for seeing the signs yet hoping for a different outcome.

Forgive yourself for things outside of your control.

Forgive yourself for missing the mark.

Forgive yourself for being prideful.

Forgive yourself for not understanding.

Forgive yourself for failing when you tried.

Forgive yourself for not seeing yourself as God sees you.

Forgive yourself for settling for less than what you deserve.

Forgive yourself now.

The Forgiving Tip #8

Your mistakes may provide a glimpse of where you're headed, but it doesn't tell the whole story. Don't allow regrets to overrule you.

Reflection Scripture

"Simon, Simon, Satan has asked to sift each of you like wheat. But I have pleaded in prayer for you, Simon, that your faith may not fail. And when you have turned back, strengthen your brothers."
Luke 22:31–32

Take A Moment

Reflect

1) I've regretted:
2) Regret no longer has power over me because:

Act

- Acknowledge the new wisdom you've gained in life from your regrets.

- Start (and continue) to be proud of yourself and the growth you've achieved in your life.

Prayer

Dear Lord,

Thank You for seeing my heart more than you see my mistakes—and loving me still. I know that I've done wrong, and I repent of my sins. I turn to You, the only One who could love and restore me like no other. Thank You for not giving up on me. Forgive me for placing my regrets over Your authority. Forgive me for falling victim to my regrets, instead of living victoriously through Your power. Please give me the wisdom to make fruitful and wise decisions. Please give me the discernment to see traps from the enemy and temptations that comes my way, no matter how subtle or innocent they may appear. You said in Your Word that when temptation comes, You have made a way of escape for me. I ask You to give me the strength to say no when my flesh desires to say yes. Please give me the desire to not only know what is right but also to act on what is right. And when I succumb to temptation and make the wrong decisions, I pray that I do not allow the enemy to have his way in my life. Remind me that my sins aren't too great for Your mercy and love. Thank You, Lord, for forgiving me and restoring me back to You.

Amen

Chapter 9

At the Cross

> *For Christ also suffered once for sin, the righteous for the unrighteous, to bring you to God. He was put to death in the body but made alive in the Spirit.*
>
> ~1 Peter 3:18

WE ALL HAVE been guilty. We've all offended and hurt someone. Whether intentional or not, big or minor, *our* actions are the reason why forgiveness has remained a struggle for some. We stand responsible for withholding apologies. We stand guilty of avoiding hard conversations. Yes, your speech and behavior has harmed those you like, love, and tolerate.

Nevertheless, if you continue to walk in victimhood and offense, you deny your role in someone's story. Like music, forgiveness and unforgiveness is a universal language that gives voice to unmet desires, fragility, and humanity. However, there's one place where both the wrongdoer and offended meet. A place where the playing field levels and where rivals become allies and victims emerge as overcomers.

That place is at the cross.

As he was dying on the cross, Jesus said, "Father forgive them, for they do not know what they are doing" (Luke 23:34). Father forgive them. His compassion for the lost moved Him to pray for them during those final moments. He could have chosen other words to say. Instead, He elected to pray for those who mocked, betrayed, and beat Him. He knew that everything in His life had led up to that moment. The time had come to glorify His Father and save the world. However, before He could become Savior, He had to encompass every aspect of a sinner.

He never played the role of victim or caused discord in His life. Nevertheless, on that day, the Peacemaker, Jesus, was accused of crimes He never committed. The One who never sinned took ownership of the sins of the world.

The selflessness and prayer Jesus displayed before those who mocked and tortured Him encourages us to follow suit—even in the most heart-wrenching circumstances. Born to reign yet called to suffer, Jesus experienced an unimaginable and terrifying death. Enduring excruciating pain and public humiliation, He knew His final hours would consist of suffering that only *He* could withstand. In His humanity, Jesus had to pay the cost for the sins of others, but in His Divinity— being God wrapped in Flesh—He understood that this journey to the cross was only the beginning. Lasting six hours, Jesus's agony on the cross was the final chapter of His physical execution. **But it wasn't the final chapter of His ministry.**

Before His birth, many prophesied of the coming Messiah. Generations heard of the One who would come to save all. Jesus was their long-awaited answer. Some expected Him to arrive with a loud fanfare and an entourage. The King of kings arrived instead as a baby, birthed in a stable in the small town of Bethlehem (see Luke 2:1–20). Because of His worthy distinction, jealousy and fear had already caught the attention of others, including King Herod, who conspired to kill Jesus in His infancy (see Matthew 2). As He grew, Jesus often taught in the synagogues, astounding adults and biblical scholars. Even as a young child, He understood His purpose, kept His focus, and humbly submitted to God while respecting His parents. Until the age of thirty He worked as a carpenter. At the time purposed by His Father, Jesus began His ministry—healing the sick, comforting the grief-stricken, and transforming the hearts of men and women.

He came for such a time as this, drawing in those whom the Father had already predestined and chosen to be His. Sent to save all, He knew the cost and impact of His sacrifice. He told His disciples, "I am the way and the truth and the life. No one comes to the Father except through me" (John 14:6). He closed the gap so that we could live and spend eternity in heaven. Salvation rested on His shoulders, and even though he understood the sacrifice it would entail, Jesus still said yes.

JOURNEY TO THE CROSS

Jesus recognized His last night with the disciples. He knew that one of them would betray Him. He understood that His miracles and teachings had all led to that moment.

> "I tell you the truth, one of you eating with me here will betray me." Greatly distressed, each one asked in turn, "Am I the one?" He replied, "It is one of you twelve who is eating from this bowl with me. For the Son of Man must die, as the Scriptures declared long ago. But how terrible it will be for the one who betrays him. It would be far better for that man if he had never been born!" (Mark 14:17–21 NLT).

Jesus, who never sinned, understood the pain of betrayal from one of His own. He knew Judas's disloyalty would set in motion what God, His Father, had planned long ago. As Jesus broke bread with the disciples, He turned to His enemy and told him, "What you are about to do, do quickly" (John 13:27).

Before Jesus was arrested and betrayed for thirty pieces of silver, He went to the Garden of Gethsemane to pray. Luke 22:44 tells us that His prayers were heartfelt and pained with the knowledge of what lay ahead: "And being in anguish, he prayed more earnestly, and his sweat was like drops of blood falling to the ground." In the moment when He asks God to change His course, we see the humanity of Jesus, but we recognize that His divinity prevailed during His moments of sorrow.

> He went on a little farther and fell to the ground. He prayed that if, it were possible, the awful hour awaiting him might pass him by. "Abba, Father," he cried out, everything is possible for you. Please take this cup of suffering away from me. Yet I want your will to be done, not mine." (Mark 14:35-36 NLT)

Jesus clearly struggled with accepting the assignment placed on Him. However, we also notice Jesus denying His flesh and feelings of turmoil in order to receive the will of His Father for His life. Jesus, fully human and fully divine, said yes to God's will, and His prayer request in the garden was denied by the only One who could help.

But as overwhelming feelings took over, He knew the assignment had His name written on it. He would not deny His Father and abandon His call. This final surrender would be extremely challenging but extremely impactful—the last act to restore man's relationship with God and send the enemy running.

God loved His Son, but someone had to pay the cost of our sin. Because of the ugliness of sin, Jesus's own Father turned His back

. . . but only for a moment. It *had* to happen. That someone who made it happen was Jesus.

He took your place. And my place. God sacrificed His only Son to save us all. God sent Him out of love, and Jesus willingly died *because* of love. "For God so loved the world that he gave his only begotten Son, that whosoever believeth in him should not perish, but have everlasting life" (John 3:16 KJV). Another classic verse from John reminds us, "Greater love hath no man than this, that a man lay down his life for his friends" (John 15:13 KJV).

Captured around midnight, guards whipped, spat, and struck Him in the face. His night was sleepless as He endured questioning and taunts. Jesus went without food and water. Over and over, He was beaten severely while His hands were tied. He could have fought back, but His silence and acceptance of what had to occur spoke louder. His skin tore from the beatings, but Jesus never said a word. Deeper layers of His skin were exposed, leaving parts of His body unrecognizable.

The Mockery & Majesty of the Cross, notes that his beatings finally stopped when they determined that He was near death. He was ultimately found guilty of blasphemy and treason and sentenced to death by crucifixion. Forced to carry His cross, Jesus made his way to Calvary (also known as Golgotha). In *The Mockery & Majesty of the Cross,* historians indicate the nails the soldiers used to nail Him to the cross ranged from 9 to 12 inches in length and were hammered into His wrists and ankles. They intended to make His death slow and painful, as it was impossible for His lungs to take a full breath. For six hours, Jesus hung on the cross with two criminals. This type of death was intended for vicious offenders, but Jesus was innocent. Even as he was dying, the crowd continued to disregard the One who could save them. *The Mockery & Majesty of the Cross* gives us further insight to consider:

They mocked His power. "Look at you now!" they yelled at him. "You said you were going to destroy the Temple and rebuild it in three days. Well then, if you are the Son of God, save yourself and come down from the cross!" (Matthew 27:40 NLT)

They mocked His name. "He trusted God, so let God rescue him now if he wants him! For he said, ' I am the Son of God.' " (Matthew 27:43 NLT)

They mocked His purpose. He saved others; himself he cannot save. If he be the king of Israel, let him now come down from the cross, and we will believe him. (Matthew 27:42 KJV).

To the bitter end, Satan wanted Jesus to forfeit His assignment, and he used the words and actions of others to taunt Him. But Jesus didn't respond with a vengeance. Instead, He prayed for them and asked God to have mercy on their souls. He *prayed* for them.

There are times when we take His sacrifice for granted. We're glad that He died for us and overjoyed that He conquered death when he resurrected from the dead three days after His crucifixion, as foretold by the prophets. **But the disconnect sometimes lies in our perception of the sins He had to bear.** *Our* **sins that** *He* **endured for us. We've glossed over our sins for far too long, accepting them as a fact of life and failing to take responsibility for them.**

For God's purpose and for reconciliation to be complete, Jesus had to be the unblemished lamb—a perfect sacrifice—to take on the sins of the world. ALL of them. When you recall your past and present sins, it's enough to make you bow your head in shame. But He carried the sins of the world. A weight unfathomable for any man to endure.

Murder, adultery, gossip, lying, jealousy, lust, gluttony, sexual perversion, backbiting, envy, slander, mockery, greed, hatred, thievery, and yes, unforgiveness—these examples of sinful behavior and speech yield "bad fruit" in our lives. They are the opposite of what God intended for us. "The Holy Spirit produces this kind of fruit in our lives: love, joy, peace, patience, kindness, goodness, faithfulness, gentleness, and self-control. There is no law against these things!" (Galatians 5:22–23 NLT). Some sins may be less noticeable than others in the beginning. However, they are still sins and ultimately hinder our growth.

I find it humbling that forgiveness, wrapped in love, is why God sent His Son. God used forgiveness as a weapon to destroy sin and restore all humanity to Himself. Because of Jesus, there's no more need for atonement through animal sacrifice, as reflected in the Old Testament. The veil and separation between God and man no longer exists. Because of the cross and His resurrection, the grip of sin no longer has us bound. In Jesus we have a new life! And through Jesus, God allows us the opportunity to belong to Him. "Therefore if any man be in Christ, he is a new creature: old things are passed away, all things have become new" (2 Corinthians 5:17 NKJV).

We are forgiven and should extend the same mercy to others.

SEEING THE TRUTH

When the Holy Spirit confronted me about forgiveness, it took some time, but I finally did answer the call. I spent many years carrying around the weight of past offenses, not fully understanding the price I was paying to remain attached to them. I made excuses, like the man at the pool of Bethesda. I didn't view rejection from a spiritual perspective. I failed to see how I helped the enemy by making pride a priority. My bitterness prevented me from believing that God had a plan, and my anger at God blocked me from growing more in faith. I didn't accept that people who are close to me were attempting to grow as well. I allowed regret to bully and blame me for things I could no longer change.

That is, until now.

This time, I want my burdens lifted so I can carry a lighter load. Life can be hard, but in hindsight, offense and pain from my past certainly made it more difficult. I carried a weight that was never mine to carry and that's offensive to Jesus, my Savior. I placed my hurt and offense above Him. I carried it around like a toddler with her favorite security blanket, clinging to it for dear life. I didn't know at the time that fear was the reason why I couldn't let go. My identity became intertwined with my pain and offense. However, after many years, I was ready for a new identity.

What did that mean for me? What did life feel like once I let it go? On the day I took the leap to forgive, I decided enough was enough. I chose to live by releasing my offenders, healing my wounds, and burying my offense. I never truly understood what others meant when they said, "Those who don't forgive have not truly understood what it means to have their sins forgiven."

I couldn't fathom how that platitude applied to me. I realize now that I hadn't entirely accepted God's forgiveness for the sins I'd committed. God never held me hostage. Instead, I kept myself bound in a prison that I'd built.

What does this mean for you?

Jesus taught about forgiveness. He demonstrated what it means to forgive, and He expects you to exhibit what He's modeled and given to you. How long will you keep holding the key to the prison you've built? How long will you carry unnecessary weight around? How many times will you replay what took place days, months, or years ago? How long will you sit with the issue and place blame? How long will you keep talking about it? How long will you cry over it? How long will you let it give you false comfort? How long will you keep score? How long will you allow the enemy to keep you in defeat? How long will you let the enemy play you like a puppet? How long will you doubt the power of Jesus? How long will you continue to allow life to pass you by? **When will you start living like an heir of Christ and choose to have joy?**

Although the offense is real and your pain is raw, what Jesus did *for* you outweighs anything that occurred *to* you. All that you've endured can't compare to the means of your freedom—the sacrificial blood of Jesus.

I acknowledged that grudges and unnecessary weight affected my mental, emotional, and spiritual outlook—even my physical health. These things were skewing my perspective and slowing down my pace rather than allowing me to soar.

No longer can you allow the enemy to bully and mentally replay what others have done to you. No longer can you maximize your offense and minimize God's power. By doing so, unforgiveness becomes the idol that you worship, granting your trials more strength and power. **I say, no more.** Instead, you must utilize your struggles and experiences as stepping stones for your future.

When I forgave and healed, *everything* looked different. No longer did I see things from the perspectives of hurt and offense. Instead, I observed things through the lens of faith, believing that God saw any hurts I endured and would do something about them.

Although the scale didn't reveal that I'd shed any pounds, I felt lighter. My steps were infused with a sense of airiness, as I experienced freedom like never before. A more genuine smile, heartier laugh, and more engagement with others had me questioning why I'd waited so long. My expressions of love became more authentic, and joy radiated from within me.

I finally made peace with my past. I am accepting people without pretense, faulty expectations, or fear of rejection. Instead of keeping score of my offenses, I keep track of my happiness. I'm not controlled by the whims of others or by the tactics of the enemy. **At last, I'm no longer on the enemy's side, because I understood that each failure to forgive is a decision to be kept in bondage.**

The enemy wants you to be ignorant of what you can have. He wants you to wallow in pity and accuse others for the rest of your life. He wants you to remain a slave to sin, never realizing that your offense—no matter its origin—prevents you from knowing who you belong to and tapping into God's power to set you free. Don't let your emotions keep you in bondage and prevent you from doing what is right. Be honest with God and tell Him all about it. God, who holds the world in His hand, can handle the pain and emotions you experience.

He wants your heart to heal more than you ever could. God desires for you to do and be all that He planned before you were in your mother's womb. Getting to the other side of forgiveness will require your willingness and cooperation. God will not do for you what *you* can do for yourself. You can take steps to forgive, and He will be there to help you walk it out.

He did it for me.

I know that He's ready and willing to do it for you.

God is your Father, defense lawyer, and your judge. He sent His Son, Jesus, to be your Savior. And we all need saving. That's what forgiveness does. It throws out the case, even when you know the other party is guilty. Forgiveness drops all charges. Forgiveness recalls the sacrifice, the torture, and humiliation Jesus endured for *your* sake.

Forgiveness calls you to grace.

Forgiveness extends mercy.

Forgiveness believes in spite of what happened.

Forgiveness loves the unlovable.

Forgiveness prays for your enemies.

Forgiveness eliminates faulty expectations.

Forgiveness receives.

Forgiveness lets go of the past and takes hold of the future.

Forgiveness gives you strength.

Forgiveness no longer dwells on bad memories.

Forgiveness is forgetting what's behind.

Forgiveness causes you to thrive in life instead of merely survive life.

Forgiveness conquers the enemy.

Forgiveness cancels your debt and the debt of others.

Forgiveness is all of that ... and then some, because forgiveness is Christ.

Forgiveness is why we're here. Because of Jesus's power, we can let it go, and our emotions become healed.

Speak to that mountain of unforgiveness.

Don't wait to forgive; have faith and forgive!

Forgive today.

Always—no matter what.

He did it for you. Do it for Him.

What's on the other side of forgiveness?
Freedom, blessings, and the love of Christ that never fails!
It's the beginning of your new life.

It's unspeakable joy, love, and peace.

It can be yours today. Always.

The choice is yours, so choose well.

It's time. It's time to give it to God and leave it there.

The Forgiving Tip #9

When you realize that Jesus's death paid for your past, current, and future sins willingly, you extend grace and erase the debts of others.

Reflection Scripture

Then Peter came to him and asked, "Lord, how often should I forgive someone who sins against me? Seven times?" "No, not seven times," Jesus replied, "but seventy times seven! Therefore, the Kingdom of Heaven can be compared to a king who decided to bring his accounts up to date with servants who had borrowed money from him. In the process, one of his debtors was brought in who owed him millions of dollars. He couldn't pay, so his master ordered that he be sold—along with his wife, his children, and everything he owned—to pay the debt. But the man fell down before his master and begged him, 'Please be patient with me, and I will pay it all.' Then his master was filled with pity for him, and he released him and forgave his debt."

Matthew 18:21–27 NLT

⟨∾ Take A Moment ∾⟩

Reflect

1) I offend and hurt Jesus when I:

2) I offend and hurt others by:

3) Grace is:

Act

- Make a numerical list of those who have offended you and why. Then list why you're forgiving them.

- Pray and look at your list as many times as you need to, as you focus on why you've decided to forgive them. Let it become engrained in your heart and mind.

Prayer

Dear Lord,

At this moment, I choose to give You my unforgiveness and wounded heart. The betrayal, rejection, wounds, bitterness, pride, excuses, and regret—Lord, I give all of these to You. Your Word says in Romans 12:1, "Offer your [body] as a living sacrifice, holy and pleasing to God—this is your true and proper worship." Lord, I give You my mind to renew and my heart to transform. I declare I will no longer view myself as a victim. I will no longer allow myself to be played like a puppet for the enemy. Lord, I release the anger, disappointments, frustrations, and "whys" I've been holding on to. I release my mental roadblocks and strongholds into Your hands, knowing that You may not have authored them but trusting that You can use all to grow and help me draw closer to You. I release offense, and I hold on to forgiveness. And I'll keep holding on to freedom. By holding on to forgiveness, I hold on to You. I honor You. I accept Your forgiveness for my sins, and I praise and worship You now and always. Thank You, Lord, for Your sacrifice. Thank You for helping me see past my pain. Thank You, Lord, for this new beginning. Amen

Congratulations, you've made the right step!

I _____, have chosen that today will be the day I say yes to forgiveness and wholeness. I understand that my decision has nothing to do with those who've offended me, past or present, or those who may offend me in the future. I choose to be intentional with my thoughts, words, and actions. I choose to be active in my healing. I choose to maximize God's power and minimize my grudges. I choose to set healthier boundaries for myself and others. I choose to let the Holy Spirit inhabit all areas of my life, and I will partner with Him each day to make it count. I choose to be free and accept His gift of love, salvation, and forgiveness. On this day, I choose to release myself and my offenders—dropping all charges. I release them into God's hands with love. I am choosing to thrive in life and help others along the way.
Thank You, Jesus, for this new day!

Date _____

THE OTHER SIDE OF FORGIVENESS

Frequently Asked Questions

As I began my journey of forgiveness and healing, I certainly had questions. I told God, "If you want me to do this, I have some questions." In a humorous but authoritative fashion, the Holy Spirit responded, "Bring it. I have the answers." I also knew that many of the following questions would resonate with you as you begin your journey. The Holy Spirit gave me answers to the most common questions I had about forgiveness and reconciliation. Those answers have been healing, and I know they will help you in your process.

- **Why should I forgive?**

While there are several reasons why you should forgive, the primary reason is that God has forgiven you. We are all sinners saved by grace. Things like sinful behaviors and thoughts that you've engaged in before and will likely engage in again need the forgiveness Christ has offered. The second reason is that, without forgiveness, you can position yourself to forfeit the benefits of living life abundantly. Unforgiveness will affect everything you do and hinder your blessings (spiritually, physically, financially, and socially) and relationships connected to you can be hindered. The question becomes, what kind of life do you want? Do you desire bondage or freedom?

"For if you forgive other people when they sin against you, your heavenly Father will also forgive you. But if you do not forgive others their sins, your Father will not forgive your sins."
Matthew 6:14-15

- **Why is it hard to forgive?**

There's no doubt about it; forgiveness can be difficult. I believe the challenge lies in confronting the hurt, pain, and betrayal that was inflicted and finding a way to let it go. Some offenses can leave us in a state of shock, because they're so unexpected. And forgiveness and emotional healing don't always happen simultaneously. Understanding that the act of forgiveness takes just a moment, whereas emotional healing can take much longer—even years—is instrumental to rising above unforgiveness.

Cast all your anxiety on him because he cares for you.
1 Peter 5:7

- **You don't understand; they don't deserve my forgiveness.**

I understand what you're saying, but we don't deserve God's forgiveness either. No one is deserving. Jesus was sinless, and He took on the sins of the world. He considered us worthy enough to pay the ultimate price for our freedom. If He can do it, so can we by His power.

"Therefore, the Kingdom of Heaven can be compared to a king who decided to bring his accounts up to date with servants who had borrowed money from him. In the process, one of his debtors was brought in who owed him millions of dollars. He couldn't pay, so his master ordered that he be sold—along with his wife, his children, and everything he owned—to pay the debt. But the man fell down before his master and begged him, 'Please be patient with me, and I will pay it all.' Then his master was filled with pity for him, and he released him and forgave his debt."
Matthew 18:23–27 NLT

- **Should I be in a relationship with them?**

Forgiveness is required; reconciliation is not. However, asking God what His will is for the relationship is key—also asking Him to help you set healthy boundaries. Some relationships, such as family relationships, may be more challenging to navigate, but all relationships need healthy boundaries. Healing takes time, and you don't have to be in a rush to "get things back to where they were." No matter what happens, your relationship can be better because you've decided to grow from what occurred.

Trust in the LORD with all your heart and lean not on your own understanding; in all your ways acknowledge Him, and He shall direct your paths.
Proverbs 3:5–6 NKJV

- **What about my enemies, what happens to them?**

Leave your enemies in God's hands and pray for them. Vengeance belongs to Him—in His way and time. Praying for your enemy is a mandate from God and will help your heart heal. The Holy Spirit will help you love them, even when you don't feel like loving them or believe that you can love them.

"You have heard that it was said, 'Love your neighbor and hate your enemy.' But I tell you, love your enemies and pray for those who persecute you, that you may be children of your Father in heaven. He causes his sun to rise on the evil and the good, and sends rain on the righteous and the unrighteous. If you love those who love you, what reward will you get?"
Matthew 5:43–46

- **Why did God let that happen?**

We've all asked that question, and we'll continue to do so. You may never understand why, and if God told you, the answer may never satisfy your question. God allowed the offense to happen for reasons we may never know. Your faith in Him can be greater than it was before. Let go of the "why" and focus on the Who. God loves you. He's faithful and He's good.

And we know that in all things God works for the good of those who love him, who have been called according to his purpose.
Romans 8:28

- **How can I stop hurting? How can I stop the pain?**

God can take the pain away instantly, or He can allow you to walk through the pain. No matter what, He's with you—every step of the way. Healing is intentional. Therefore, partnering with God will certainly help you heal and forgive. Release your hurt to God and ask Him to help you stop recycling the memories. Seeking help from a competent counselor can also benefit you during this time. Seek Him out on how you should proceed.

"Come to me, all you who are weary and burdened, and I will give you rest. Take my yoke upon you and learn from me, for I am gentle and humble in heart, and you will find rest for your souls. For my yoke is easy and my burden is light."
Matthew 11:28–30

- **What about those who've offended me?**

I'm not giving them the benefit of the doubt, but you don't know what God is doing in their life. Sometimes it's hard to believe that God cares about your offender as He cares about you. Continue to pray for them and release them to God.

"But I tell you who hear me: Love your enemies, do good to those who hate you, bless those who curse you, pray for those who mistreat you."
Luke 6:27–28

- **What happens if I don't forgive?**

By choosing *not* to forgive, you are placing yourself above God, and you stand in your own way. You become a prisoner to what happened, and you won't soar or reach your full potential. You will negatively impact your family generationally and open the door to physical ailments, spiritual attacks, mental roadblocks, and more. Do yourself a favor and forgive.

"I am the LORD your God, who brought you out of Egypt, out of the land of slavery. You shall have no other gods before me. You shall not make for yourself an image in the form of anything in heaven above or on the earth beneath or in the waters below. You shall not bow down to them or worship them; for I the LORD your God, am a jealous God, punishing the children for the sin of the fathers to the third and fourth generation of those who hate me, but showing love to a thousand generations of those who love me and keep my commandments."
Deuteronomy 5:6–10

- **I need or want an apology. Shouldn't they apologize first before I forgive?**

Apologies are nice, but they're not required. Taking ownership of what you choose to hold on to or release will be the key to gaining and maintaining your freedom. If you have been offended by another Christian, the Bible tells us how to approach and handle difficult conversations (see Matthew 18:15–17). Before confronting them, pray about it. God's peace is a good indicator of the discussion and the timing of it. The Holy Spirit can give you a strategy on how to approach them and how to heal.

Do not repay anyone evil for evil. Be careful to do what is right in the eyes of everyone. If it is possible, as far as it depends on you, live at peace with everyone. Do not take revenge, my dear friends, but leave room for God's wrath, for it is written: "It is mine to avenge; I will repay," says the Lord. On the contrary: "If your enemy is hungry, feed him; if he is thirsty, give him something to drink. In doing this, you will heap burning coals on his head." Do not be overcome by evil but overcome evil with good.
Romans 12:17–21

- **How can what has happened work for my good?**

Romans 8:28 tells us that all things work together for good. That should give us hope. We may never know how or when things can work out in the end. However, when you continue to put your trust in God, you can rest assured that your experience will not be wasted.

The LORD makes firm the steps of the one who delights in him; though he stumble, he will not fall, for the LORD upholds him with his hand.
Psalm 37:23–24

- **How do I move past this?**

One day at a time. The Bible provides so many reasons why focusing on the day you're given should be your priority. New mercies and new grace are given to you . . . one day at a time.

"This, then, is how you should pray: 'Our Father in heaven, hallowed be your name, your kingdom come, your will be done on earth as it is in heaven, Give us today our daily bread. Forgive us our debts, as we also have forgiven our debtors.' "
Matthew 6:9–12

- **But I see them every day. That makes it harder for me to forgive and heal.**

Forgiveness and healing can be more challenging when the one who's caused you harm is staring you in the face—daily. But the outcome remains the same. Ask God for help, pray for yourself, and release them to God.

Do not repay evil with evil or insult with insult, but with a blessing, because to this you were called so that you may inherit a blessing.
1 Peter 3:9

- **My friends and family were supposed to be there. They hurt and disappointed me. How can I trust them again?**

Even well-meaning and loving family members or friends can disappoint. All relationships disappoint in some way. God is the only One who can be trusted wholeheartedly. There's no guarantee it won't happen again. However, you can set expectations, and trust can be rebuilt, slowly and surely. Seek God on how to move forward with them.

Though my father and mother forsake me, the Lord will receive me.
Psalm 27:10

- **Are some people or situations easier to forgive than others?**

It may appear that way. I've heard of situations so horrific that they seem nearly impossible to forgive. Nonetheless, those individuals chose to set themselves and their perpetrators free by way of forgiveness. At the same time, I've witnessed those who've faced less tragic circumstances than others withhold forgiveness. Forgiveness is an individual choice. No matter what happened, it's all placed at the foot of the cross.

"Behold, I am the LORD, the God of all flesh. Is there anything too hard for me?
Jeremiah 32:27 KJV

- **How can I avoid being hurt?**

You were not made to go through life dodging hurt. You can't. You're human, and things happen. Even Jesus faced betrayal by Judas, one of His chosen disciples. Taking steps to set healthy boundaries can prevent *some* offenses from occurring or lessen their blow. Going through life with a wall built around your heart and trying to avoid pain will keep you in bondage. Don't let that happen. Don't let fear prevent you from engaging in life and with others. You deserve better than that.

Two are better than one, because they have a good return for their labor: If either of them falls down, one can help the other up. But pity anyone who falls and has no one to help them up.
Ecclesiastes 4:8–10

- **I know I've hurt others; how can I make things right again?**

Sometimes you'll have the opportunity to apologize immediately for an offense and receive forgiveness on the spot, but that's not always a common scenario. If time has passed, pray first before you go back and apologize. Praying for yourself and the person you've offended can initiate healing and reconciliation (if reconciliation is God's will). God can position their heart to help them be receptive to you and your heartfelt apology. He can also help them get emotionally ready for dialogue. While they may or may not accept your apology, making the first step to correct your wrong is the right thing to do. Both parties are responsible for taking ownership of apologies and acceptance.

"If your brother or sister sins against you, go point out their fault, just between the two of you. If they listen to you, you have won them over. But if they will not listen, take one or two others along, so that 'every matter may be established by the testimony of two or three witnesses.' If they still refuse to listen, tell it to the church;

and if they refuse to listen even to the church, treat him as you would a pagan or a tax collector."
Matthew 18:15–17

- **How many times should I forgive them?**

Continuously. Every day and at every opportunity that comes up. Although the following scripture provides an actual number of times you should forgive, this number represents that forgiveness is ongoing and limitless.

Then Peter came to Jesus and asked, "Lord, how many times shall I forgive my brother or sister who sins against me? Up to seven times?" Jesus answered, "I tell you, not seven times, but seventy-seven times."
Matthew 18:21–22

- **Is unforgiveness a sin?**

Yes. Unforgiveness is prideful and rebellious, which goes against who God is and all that He stands for.

"And when you stand praying, if you hold anything against anyone, forgive him, so that your Father in heaven may forgive you your sins."
Mark 11:25–26

- **Can you fully accept Christ's forgiveness and still withhold forgiveness from others?**

I believe withholding forgiveness demonstrates that individuals may not have a real understanding of Christ's sacrifice. I question if that person truly believes that God has forgiven *them* of their sins. When you realize how much you are forgiven, you forgive.

If anyone says, "I love God," and hates his brother, he is a liar; for he who does not love his brother whom he has seen cannot love God whom he has not seen. And this commandment we have from him: whoever loves God must also love his brother.
1 John 4:20–21 ESV

- **The memories won't stop. How do I make them go away?**

The enemy would love for you to replay what happened, and your mind has a great recall ability. Being intentional about stopping the replay is critical. It's not a matter of if, but when. Anything can trigger memories about the details of an offense and the emotions that come with it. However, you can put an end to harmful recurring memory immediately. By choosing not to dwell on them and asking God to renew your mind continually, you can gain control of your thoughts. Think about what you're thinking about. Is it good? Is it an asset or a liability to your personal growth?

Therefore, I urge you, brothers and sisters, in view of God's mercy, to offer your bodies as a living sacrifice, holy and pleasing to God— this is your true and proper worship. Do not conform to the pattern of this world, but be transformed by the renewing of your mind. Then you will be able to test and approve what God's will is—his good, pleasing and perfect will.
Romans 12:1–2

- **I pray to forgive and nothing happens. What should I do?**

Keep praying. Remain steadfast in faith. Along with intentionality, it takes faith to forgive. Forgiveness doesn't just happen. Over time, you'll notice that it gets better.

Then Jesus told his disciples a parable to show them that they should always pray and not give up. He said: "In a certain town there was a judge who neither feared God nor cared about men. And there was a widow in that town who kept coming to him with the plea, 'Grant me justice against my adversary.' For some time he refused. But finally he said to himself, 'Even though I don't fear God or care about men, yet because this widow keeps bothering me, I will see that she gets justice, so that she won't eventually come and attack me!'" And the Lord said, "Listen to what the unjust judge says. And will not God bring about justice for his chosen ones, who cry out to him day and night? Will he keep putting them off?"
Luke 18:1–7

- **After everything that's happened, how do I let the past go?**

You let go by faith. You decide that your future is worth fighting for and become active in taking the right steps (prayer, extra support, and transforming your mind and heart). You partner with God to make it happen instead of waiting for God to make things happen.

But don't just listen to God's word. You must do what it says. Otherwise, you are only fooling yourselves. For if you listen to the

word and don't obey, it is like glancing at your face in a mirror. You see yourself, walk away, and forget what you look like. But if you look carefully into the perfect law that sets you free, and if you do what it says and don't forget what you heard, then God will bless you for doing it.
James 1:22–25 NLT

- **I know that I've hurt God with my sins. Will Christ forgive me?**

You're not alone. We have all fallen short and are in need of forgiveness—every day. Yes, Christ can and will forgive you. His forgiveness does not make you exempt from consequences. However, His forgiveness is available to you. Repent and ask Him to forgive you. Ask Him to make your sins as white as snow. Turn to Him and believe that your request is received, and His answer is, "Yes, I forgive you and I love you."

"Come now, and let us reason together," says the LORD. *"Though your sins are like scarlet, they shall be as white as snow; though they are red as crimson, they shall be as wool."*
Isaiah 1:18 NKJV

- **How do I know that Christ has forgiven me? It doesn't feel like He has.**

Don't allow the enemy to make you believe that your sin is too bad for God's forgiveness. It's not. When you repent and ask for forgiveness, believe it. Sin no more and keep moving forward.

The LORD is compassionate and gracious, slow to anger, abounding in love. He will not always accuse, nor will he harbor his anger forever; he does not treat us as our sins deserve or repay us according to our iniquities. For as high as the heavens are above the earth, so great is his love for those who fear him; as far as the east is from the west, so far has he removed our transgressions from us.
Psalm 103:8–12

NOTES

Introduction

1. *Merriam Webster Dictionary, www.merriam-webster.com.*

Chapter 5: When You've Been Dropped

1. *Merriam Webster Dictionary, www.merriam-webster.com.*

Chapter 7: When It Doesn't Make Sense

1. *NLT, Life Application Study Bible* (Wheaton, IL: Tyndale House Publishers, Inc., 2004), 784.

Chapter 9: At The Cross

1. Bill Crowder, *The Mockery and Majesty of the Cross* (Grand Rapids, MI: RBC Ministries, 2008), 8, 14-1

ACKNOWLEDGEMENTS

To my parents, Robert and Teresa Seals, your unconditional love and support continue to amaze me. God blessed me beyond what I could ever want and imagine when He gave me you. Thank you for showing me how to love, forgive, and stay focused on the task at hand- among other things. You have supported and encouraged me in writing this book. You have instilled an attitude of gratefulness and success, that continues to unfold in my life. You continue to believe in me, and the dreams God has for my life. I love you to no end.

To my sister, Landria Green, thank you for your support, love, and direction. I could not have asked for a better sister to have on this journey. You encourage me to continue recognizing the greatness within. I'm so thankful for our relationship, and your sense of humor is always on time.

To my editor, Ashley Casteel, your expertise was a Godsend. I'm so glad that He connected us, for such a time as this. Thank you for your encouragement and for helping me take this message to the world.

To my Savior, Jesus Christ. Without you, I am nothing. Thank you for healing my heart and walking this process of forgiveness out. Thank you for transforming my life and thank you for using me to reach those you've predestined. Words can never convey the love I have for you. I honor and worship You, all the days of my life. Thank you for loving me.

About the Author

Dionnea Seals (www.dionneaseals.com) is a Licensed Professional Counselor, National Board-Certified Counselor, Speaker, Author, and Doctoral student - who has a heart for sharing the Gospel and helping others thrive. She is the founder of Encouraging Hearts, Inspiring Minds- a ministry and website that provides inspirational posts from a Christian perspective. Dionnea is also the founder and CEO for Gabuchi Publishing House and podcast host for, Dionnea Speaks: Helping you apply God's Truth to your everyday. Dionnea has served as Youth Director in ministry for 4.5 years and Christian education facilitator for youth and adult conferences. Connect with Dionnea on her website and social media.

Instagram: dionneaseals

Facebook: asinglemomentd

For bookings or inquiries, contact Gabuchi Publishing House: gpublishinghouse@gmail.com

THANKS FOR READING!

Please add a review on Amazon, I'd love to know your thoughts about the book. Amazon reviews are helpful for authors and your support is appreciated. Share your review on social media and use the hashtag #TOF and encourage others to read too!

www.ingramcontent.com/pod-product-compliance
Lightning Source LLC
Chambersburg PA
CBHW070600010526
44118CB00012B/1401